An Evaluation of Postal Service Wage Rates

An Evaluation of Postal Service Wage Rates

Douglas K. Adie

With a foreword by Yale Brozen

American Enterprise Institute for Public Policy Research
Washington, D.C.

Douglas K. Adie is a member of the Department of Economics at Ohio University.

Library of Congress Cataloging in Publication Data

Adie, Douglas K
    An evaluation of Postal Service wage rates.

    (AEI studies; 166)
    1. Postal service—United States—Salaries, pensions, etc. I. Title. II. Series:
American Enterprise Institute for Public Policy Research. AEI studies; 166.
HE6499.A6   331.2'81'3834973   77-14355
ISBN 0-8447-3265-6

AEI Studies 166

Printed in the United States of America

CONTENTS

FOREWORD

That the U.S. Postal Service delivers as much mail as quickly as it does is the eighth wonder of the world, not because it does the task well but that it gets the job done at all. In the face of an organizational structure that gives supervisors responsibility with little authority and a pay structure that rewards people more for seniority than for skill or productivity, the accomplishment of its work is a minor miracle.

The Post Office Department was reorganized into the U.S. Postal Service in 1970-1971 with great hopes that replacing the patronage system for selecting postal management with a career system containing some elements of professionalism would revolutionize efficiency. What was left out was an incentive system for motivating efficient accomplishment. In one of its first steps in 1970 before actually taking command of the facilities of the Post Office Department in 1971, the U.S. Postal Service management negotiated an agreement with the postal unions that actually reduced the already minimal incentives for employees to assume responsibility, take initiative, or improve their skill. It agreed to a compression of the pay structure and provided for what amounted to additional pay increases on top of the 14 percent increase that had just been granted to buy union agreement to the reorganization of the Post Office. What little incentive for performance had existed in the pay structure was drained by this move. That any increase in productivity has occurred since is the ninth wonder of the world.

The payroll costs of the Post Office Department were excessive before the U.S. Postal Service took command and replaced congressional wage setting with collective bargaining. Budgets for postal personnel were strained by rates of pay that, on the average, were 10 to 20 percent too high. The average encompassed pay rates that were probably too low in Chicago and New York, at least in 1966 and in

1970, and 30 to 40 percent too high in small towns and rural areas. Since collective bargaining with the U.S. Postal Service has begun, postal pay rates have escalated, rising more rapidly than wage rates in the rest of the economy. The U.S. Postal Service has bought peace with its unions at a cost to postal patrons and taxpayers of well over $2 billion a year. This is equivalent to adding four cents an ounce to first-class postage. Where postal wage rates once exceeded general pay levels by 25 percent, they now exceed general pay levels by 35 percent. The Council on Wage and Price Stability table shown below gives some indication of this behavior.

What is to be done to improve productivity and restrain excessive pay increases in the U.S. Postal Service? Professor Adie suggests a number of improvements in pay structure (including the use of different rates of pay in different labor markets), recruiting practices, employee training, and physical facilities. But these steps can accomplish little without fundamental changes in incentives. To accomplish this, Professor Adie recommends the repeal of the Private Express Statutes that grant the U.S. Postal Service a monopoly of first-class mail.

Failing repeal, Professor Adie suggests that Congress empower the Postal Rate Commission to refuse to grant any increases in postal rates to cover wage increases granted when the voluntary quit rate in the Postal Service is less than 12 percent per year. This, he estimates,

AVERAGE HOURLY EARNINGS FOR NONSUPERVISORY WORKERS IN THE PRIVATE NONFARM ECONOMY AND AVERAGE HOURLY PAY FOR POSTAL WORKERS[a]

	Hourly Earnings[b]			Percent Change		
	1970	1973	1975	1970-1973	1973-1975	1970-1975
Postal workers	$4.05	$4.95	$6.11	22.2	23.4	50.9
Private nonfarm economy	3.23	3.90	4.53	20.7	16.2	40.2

a Average hourly pay for postal workers does not include overtime, while average hourly earnings data for the private nonfarm economy does. Our review of the Postal Service's National Payroll Hours Summary Report for Accounting Period I, FY 1976, indicates that 4 percent of clerks' pay was at overtime rates. Hence, including overtime would increase Postal Service hourly earnings slightly.

b Figures for July of each year.

Source: U.S. Postal Service, Bureau of Labor Statistics, *Employment and Earnings*, Table C-2.

would still result in wage rates excessive, on the *average*, by 20 percent. This, of course, fails to do anything about the lack of incentives or perverse incentives for efficiency and touches only one aspect of the problem of excessive costs. It is only one small step, but at least it is a step in the right direction.

YALE BROZEN
Graduate School of Business
University of Chicago

INTRODUCTION

When in 1968 the Kappel Commission concluded "the most searching and exhaustive review ever undertaken" of postal affairs, it recommended the reorganization of the Post Office Department into a quasi-independent government corporation. Legislation to effect this change was passed in 1970. The new body, named the U.S. Postal Service, began operating July 1, 1971. It is doubtful that a study of the Postal Service today, even if it were as comprehensive as the Kappel Commission report, would add much to our knowledge. While reorganization changed the name, structure, and some of the higher level administrative channels, the day-to-day operations, incentive system, and *modus operandi* of the service have remained almost intact.

This study has a narrower objective. It evaluates the average wage level paid by the Post Office and the Postal Service to nonsupervisory employees. The conclusions possible are that wages are about

The execution of this study has been solely my own, and for its opinions I take full responsibility. Many others, however, have contributed to the undertaking. I have been assisted by Jean Lee, Janet Bolen, and Laura Genero at the American Enterprise Institute in Washington. Computational assistance was rendered by Gary Wheeler and Kit Yee Lim. Marie Frontera and Stephanie Goldsberry typed the manuscript.

I am grateful to some of the most knowledgeable and competent people in the fields of labor economics and postal affairs, who commented, sometimes extensively, on the manuscript at various stages. For this chore my thanks go to Yale Brozen, John Haldi, Tom Johnson, H. Gregg Lewis, Albert Rees, and Tim Wheeler. This study has been much improved by their labors.

I have also benefited from the comments and suggestions of numerous postal officials, most of whom prefer to remain anonymous; of persons attending the Labor Workshop at the University of Chicago and the Small Group Session in the College of Business Administration at Ohio University; and of several colleagues in the Department of Economics at Ohio University, especially Steve Pejovich and Ismail Ghazalah.

right, too low, or excessive. The study treats only incidentally such internal functions of the Postal Service as mail transportation, research, engineering, organization and administration, and the external relationships of the Postal Service with other elements of the postal complex. Problems of wage structure, financial management, costing, pricing of different types of mail, and efficient mail delivery are also treated peripherally in connection with the wage determination process.

In chapter 1, the commission of the Post Office and the Postal Service is examined in historical context to determine if there has been sufficient incentive for postal executives to pay optimal wages. The answer is no. The present internal operations of the Postal Service are briefly discussed, providing further qualitative evidence on this question both before and after the reorganization. The finding is that reorganization has not solved the basic problem of incentive and that postal workers continue to be overpaid, in most areas of the country and in the most populous postal occupations.

Chapter 2 describes the wage determination process and the wage structure resulting from it. The postal labor unions, which participate strongly in the wage determination process, have considerable experience, expertise, and strength in lobbying and working with Congress. They have usually been successful in realizing their demands. Chapter 2 also examines employees' working conditions, since these offer nonpecuniary benefits to postal workers and constitute a portion of their compensation.

Chapter 3 analyzes the relationship between wage rates and the voluntary quit rate in the context of business operations. Inadequate pay or promotions being the most important reasons for workers quitting, we must postulate a strong inverse relationship between a firm's wage rate and its quit rate. The empirical analysis of the Post Office/Postal Service wage rates begins in 1958 because it has not been possible to collect quit rate data for the Post Office before then. The chapter concludes with an estimate of the parameters of a relationship between the wage rate and the quit rate for the Post Office and Postal Service over the period 1958-1972.

In chapter 4 the "prevailing wage principle" and the "cost of living model" are rejected as techniques for evaluating wages because of their imprecision and biases. A specific human capital model is developed that relies on the inverse relationship between quit and wage rates in an industry and on the fact that specific human capital is lost when workers quit. An optimal wage is calculated to minimize total labor costs, which consist of wages and the loss of specific human capital from quits for a given-size labor force. This optimal wage for an industry is then expressed in an operational form that depends on the parameters of the quit–wage rate relationship and an estimate of the average value of specific human capital losses.

There follows in chapter 5 a review of some of the work that has attempted to calculate the costs of recruiting, hiring, and training a worker to replace one who quits. Financial and descriptive data are used to estimate the probable range of personnel costs per new recruit for the Postal Service. These are, in short, estimates of the value of specific human capital invested by the Postal Service in its nonsupervisory employees.

Using the expression for optimal wages along with the values of the parameters for the quit–wage rate relationship postulated in Appendix A and the estimates of personnel costs contained in chapter 5, optimal wage rates for the Postal Service are calculated for each of the years 1958-1972 and discussed in chapter 6. Also discussed in this chapter are the probable reasons for the excessive wages paid Postal Service employees.

Chapter 7 considers a regional differential wage structure suggested by the optimal wage model. New policies are proposed to deal with the problem of excessive wages, while recognizing possible exceptions within the Postal Service.

The Kappel report describes the Post Office before reorganization. Some inefficiencies appear to have been removed as a result of reorganization; others, however, have been fostered. Worse yet, the Postal Service has failed to overcome many of the problems that prompted reorganization. In discussing the situation in the Post Office Department before reorganization and the Postal Service since reorganization, the aim of this study is to describe the reasons for the wage premiums paid postal workers in these two periods. In some respects, the reasons for these wage premiums differed, but in many respects they produced similar results. The findings of this study suggest that postal workers continue to be overpaid since reorganization as they were before, in most areas of the country and in the most populous postal occupations.

1

THE HISTORY OF
THE U. S. POSTAL SERVICE

By any measure the U.S. Postal Service is an enormous enterprise. It is among the largest employers in the world, with a work force of almost 700,000 processing 90 billion pieces of mail each year. It is the nation's largest user of floor space: it owns 3,000 facilities with 60 million square feet, and leases 26,000 facilities with 72 million square feet, for a total of 132 million square feet—about 5 square miles of floor space. It is the nation's largest nonmilitary purchaser of transport and operates more than 200,000 vehicles—more than the top five commercial carriers combined. It maintains over 300,000 streetcorner mailboxes, sells enough stamps to stretch around the world eighteen times, and handles half the world's mail—enough to fill 400,000 boxcars each year. (A train with 400,000 cars would reach from coast to coast and then some.) It is designed to make deliveries to every office and residence in America every day, six days a week. Its rural carriers alone travel over 2 million miles each day (four round trips to the moon), and its city carriers walk or drive another million miles a day. Its operating budget in 1976 was over $14 billion, which approaches 1 percent of the gross national product.

The most startling aspect of these vast statistics is that they have been amassed, for all practical purposes, with hand labor. Year after year the Postal Service devotes 85 percent of its budget to its payroll, and only 15 percent to equipment, offices, transportation, fuel, and other capital costs. Plans to modernize and mechanize postal operations have never lived up to expectations, and it remains about as labor intensive as ever. In fact, one could reasonably doubt that the Postal Service shows any great advances over the capital structure of pyramid building in Egypt.

In this context the question of postal wage excesses takes on a

1

new meaning. Hand labor is inherently inefficient. To overpay the immense Postal Service labor force is to multiply the inefficiency of its operations. If this study is correct in its conclusions that postal workers are overpaid by as much as one-third, the American public is paying dearly for permitting the king's postal monopoly, little changed, to crawl towards the twenty-first century.

Commission and Development of the Post Office

In 1775 because of the trend toward war, the Continental Congress sought to establish a secure mail delivery organization to maintain communication between the states and to supply revenue for the army. It was not until 1782 that Congress gave the federal government "sole and exclusive" postal power, and when the Constitution was ratified in 1789 this was omitted. Article I, section 8, of the United States Constitution reads: "The Congress shall have the power . . . to regulate commerce with foreign nations and among the several states . . . [and] to establish post offices and post roads." The Constitution does not authorize a postal monopoly. However, Congress reenacted the 1782 statute giving the government a postal monopoly by legislative mandate. Article IX of the Articles of Confederation gave Congress "the sole and exclusive right and power of . . . establishing and regulating post offices from one State to another . . . and exacting such postage on papers passing through the same as may be requisit to defray the expenses of the said office. . . ."

These provisions established in 1789 a self-financing, independent postal system for the United Colonies. The Continental Congress, while legislating a monopoly for interstate postal service was little concerned about private competition. Its interest lay in creating a dependable service. Postmaster General Benjamin Franklin and his successor, Samuel Osgood, both exemplified this view and busied themselves with the practical matter of providing good postal services across a vast, little-tamed land.[1]

Legislative development since the Continental Congress has been in a protectionist direction despite the views of the first two postmasters. An act of 1792 made illegal the establishment of a private postal service "whereby the revenue of the general Post Office may be injured." Despite this act, entrepreneurs, encouraged by high postage rates, employed agents to carry letters by rail and wiped out two-

---

[1] Morton S. Baratz, *The Economics of the Postal Service* (Washington, D.C.: Public Affairs Press, 1962), p. 44. See also John Haldi, *Postal Monopoly* (Washington, D.C.: American Enterprise Institute, 1974), pp. 1-28.

thirds of the federal business on key routes between 1840 and 1844. The courts pointed out that this practice was lawful and juries refused to indict offenders. It was not until March 3, 1845, that Congress responded to this practice by passing a new act making it unlawful to establish any "private express" for the conveyance of "letters . . . or other mail." By 1860 the postal monopoly was confirmed by judicial decision and in 1872 an ordinance reserved to Congress the sole and exclusive right to establish and regulate post offices. In 1948 the Private Express Statutes, which contain the provisions for the existing postal monopoly, were recodified as part of Title 18 of the United States Code.

The concept of public service was joined to the postal monopoly in the nineteenth century when the Post Office was developing links between different parts of the country. The Congress later authorized the parcel post service[2] and gave the Post Office a number of new service functions. Some of these, such as the postal money order system and the savings deposit system, competed with private enterprise. The Postal Policy Act of 1958 confirmed that the Post Office was a public service. More recently, James H. Rademacher, president of the National Association of Letter Carriers, stated that "the post office is and always must be a service to all the American people; it is not a money-making scheme. It is not a public utility."

This was not the policy intended by the framers of the Constitution or the early organizers and postmasters.[3] The Postal Reorganization Act, by downgrading the public service aspects and requiring that postal costs fall on the users of mail in proportion to their use, rather than on the Treasury, has, in principle at least, moved the Postal Service closer to the intentions of founders of the Post Office.

The Privileges of the Postal Service

The Postal Service enjoys three privileges that enable it to raise its revenues above what they would be under competitive conditions. These privileges are: (1) an exemption from corporation, property, and business taxes; (2) a legal monopoly on first-class letters that permits it to set rates much higher than would otherwise be possible; and (3) a subsidy from Congress to compensate it for public service costs and for losses. The Postal Service's exemption from corporation,

---

[2] Kappel Commission, *Towards Postal Excellence*, Report of the President's Commission on Postal Organization, vol. 1, 1968, Washington, D.C., p. 9.

[3] John Haldi, *Postal Monopoly*, p. 7.

property, and business taxes gives it a strong advantage over all private competitors. This advantage makes it more difficult for entrepreneurs to compete with the Postal Service in areas of its operations where there are no barriers to entry (all classes of mail except first).

A legal monopoly for the Postal Service is defended with two arguments. One is that the Postal Service is a natural monopoly as a consequence of economies of scale and can, therefore, provide postal service for the entire country more efficiently than any group of smaller firms. Postmaster General Bailar used this argument to justify the postal monopoly when he said the Postal Service's 30,000 post offices make it the most efficient carrier. This argument is specious. A natural monopolist does not need legal protection. If a business enjoys increasing returns to scale—and it is far from obvious that the Postal Service does—it can make the market unattractive to competitors and would-be entrants by providing a superior service at a cheaper price while still earning a profit. If it cannot do this, then legal monopoly protection is pernicious. When competitors are banned from the market, it is the *public* that requires protection from exploitation by the monopolist, not the other way around. The natural monopoly argument, then, is not an acceptable justification for the legal protection given to the Postal Service.

The second argument for the postal monopoly is that, in the absence of a legal monopoly, private firms would take the most profitable or lucrative business and leave the Postal Service with the least profitable business. This has, in fact, happened several times in America. The argument implicitly concedes that under the existing rate structure there is "cream to be skimmed." In other words, some mail users are presently being overcharged. Rather than being labeled "cream skimmers," competitors who attract the most lucrative business with better service at lower rates are protecting consumers from price gouging and should be encouraged. Instead of supporting the legal status of the monopoly, this argument calls for its abolition.[4]

The privilege of a subsidy from Congress for the Postal Service is also justified on two grounds. The first is that the payment is not a subsidy but a fee for numerous miscellaneous federal services provided at local post offices. Post offices act as depositories of flags for veterans' funerals, assist in the collection of revenue for the Customs Bureau, post FBI wanted posters, distribute federal income tax and alien registration forms, and sell migratory bird-hunting stamps. The second justification for subsidization is that the Postal Service operates

---

[4] Alan Reynolds, "A Kind Word for 'Cream Skimming,'" *Harvard Business Review*, vol. 52 (November-December 1974), pp. 113-20.

under numerous constraints imposed by Congress that make it to some degree a public service operation. The Postal Policy Act of 1958 designates the following as "public service" areas:

- mail handled free or at reduced postage rates, particularly mail of nonprofit organizations, books, magazines, pamphlets, and newspapers;
- the transporting of U.S. mail by foreign air carriers;
- the star route system and third- and fourth-class post offices; and
- special services such as money orders, special delivery, and COD.

Since the size of the subsidy was supposed to be based on the costs of providing these services, the method of measuring them was important to the Post Office for revenue. In 1962 the measurement of public service was changed from a "revenue forgone" basis to a "total loss" basis. This increased the subsidy for certain public service activities in 1963 from $73 million to $206 million. By 1967, the subsidy for identified public services passed a half billion dollars: $25.8 million for nonpostal services performed for other government agencies and minor amounts of government mail, $108.1 million for rural operations, and $433.1 million for deficits incurred in connection with free and reduced-rate mail.

Under the Postal Reorganization Act the government still subsidizes the Postal Service in three ways. The first is a public service subsidy for the provision of effective and regular postal services in rural areas and small communities nationwide. This subsidy was set at $920 million a year—10 percent of the total Post Office appropriation in fiscal year 1971—and is to continue until 1979. After 1979 it is to be reduced by $92 million each year until 1984. After 1984 the Postal Service may reduce the amount requested if the funds are no longer required.

The second is a subsidy for revenue forgone—that is, not received as a result of providing reduced-rate mail service to newspaper and magazine publishers, certain nonprofit organizations, and the blind. The Postal Service determines the amount of the revenue loss and receives an annual appropriation from Congress for this amount. Some portion of the revenue-forgone subsidy is being phased out by raising the rates charged publishers in annual steps to the level of their costs. Another portion, which is to continue, reimburses the Postal Service for mandated free services and for those postage rates that must by statute be set at reduced levels to cover only attributable costs, not institutional costs. Since the attributable costs as calculated

5

by the Postal Rate Commission are about 60 percent of total costs, a significant portion of the subsidy in this category will remain.

The third kind of subsidy is for the transitional costs of reorganizing the Post Office Department into the Postal Service. In 1973 the Post Office Department's liability for annual leave earned but not used and for workmen's compensation paid under this provision was $32.5 million. This subsidy was augmented by approximately $108 million in 1973 and $114 million in 1974 to help the Postal Service meet its obligation to the Civil Service Retirement and Disability Fund. The Supplemental Appropriations Act of 1974 provided an additional subsidy of $105 million for revenue forgone and $220 million to offset the effect of a Cost of Living Council order delaying the implementation of the 1974 temporary rate increases. In 1976 Congress provided another $1 billion in aid for the service, but imposed a temporary moratorium on rate hikes (P.L. 94-421).

While reorganization was intended to lead to the elimination of the Postal Service's dependency on the general Treasury, in fact, subsidies have been higher since reorganization than before, averaging $1.4 billion in the 1969-1971 period and $1.5 billion in the 1972-1975 period (see Table 1). In fiscal years 1974 and 1975, despite higher subsidies and higher rates, operating expenses exceeded total income by $500 million and $1 billion, respectively. Thus the Postal Service has had to borrow in those years to help meet current operating expenses.

The Postal Reorganization Act authorizes the Postal Service to issue and sell obligations secured by a first lien on its receipts and guaranteed by the federal government up to a limit of $10 billion total with a yearly limitation of $2 billion, of which not more than $500 million may be used to cover operating expenses. The service has currently $1,125 million of debt incurred to meet operating expenses. As of September 30, 1978, it is expected that outstanding indebtedness will amount to $4.5 billion, $1.7 billion of which will occur in fiscal 1978. The Postal Service can continue to charge large losses against its equity by borrowing to replenish its current assets—but this would be to court bankruptcy or force an increase in the borrowing limit. Before the Economics Club of Detroit on March 8, 1976, Postmaster General Bailar stated that the Postal Service faces a "financial crisis" and is "heading for a potential disaster." By 1984 he predicts the Postal Service will be bankrupt unless major actions are taken to correct the situation. The service is more likely to try to raise additional revenue for wage increases through higher rates on first-class mail and through additional subsidies.

Table 1

SUMMARY OF UNITED STATES POSTAL SERVICE FINANCES, FISCAL YEARS ENDING JUNE 30
($ thousands)

	1975	1974	1973	1972ᵃ	1971	1970	1969
Operating revenue	$10,015,170	$ 9,008,314	$8,388,945	$7,884,188	$6,664,988	$6,346,655	$6,142,234
Government appropriationsᵇ	1,532,934	1,750,445	1,485,595	1,424,191	2,086,496	1,355,040	883,664
Total income	11,548,104	10,758,759	9,824,540	9,308,379	8,751,484	7,701,695	7,025,898
Salaries and benefits	10,805,408	9,641,557	8,450,914	8,145,538	7,467,036	6,524,819	5,901,340
Other expenses	1,768,797	1,653,782	1,475,527	1,439,831	1,488,228	1,342,450	1,267,149
Total operating expenses	12,574,205	11,295,339	9,926,441	9,585,369	8,955,264	7,867,269	7,168,489
Operating loss	1,026,101	536,580	101,901	276,990	203,780	165,374	142,591
Other income, net	37,343	98,221	88,937	101,555			
Net Loss	$ 988,758	$ 438,358	$ 12,964	$ 175,435	$ 203,780	$ 165,574	$ 142,591

ᵃ This is the first U.S. Postal Service budget. The U.S. Postal Service was established July 1, 1971. Financial statements prior to that date are those of the Post Office Department. Such statements for 1969-1971 have been restated above to be in a format generally consistent with 1972-1975.

ᵇ Before fiscal year 1972, government appropriations were made to cover the entire POD operations and capital commitments.

Source: *Annual Reports of the Postmaster General, 1972-1973,* p. 43; *1973-1974,* p. 47; *1974-1975,* p. 49.

The Problem of Incentive

Despite what postal executives say, the incentives operating within the system are not likely to induce the Postal Service to minimize costs and to end its dependency on government subsidies. Indeed, since the service operates under a zero-profit rule, there is no reward or incentive for minimizing costs. The Postal Service cannot pay profits to stockholders and it is postal policy, specified in the reorganization act, not to earn a surplus. In the days of the old Post Office Department, whenever surpluses were earned, they were "confiscated" in the form of lowered subsidies or lowered rates. This would probably happen under the new organization too. Consequently, the goal of the Postal Service is only to break even and perhaps retain a small contingency fund.[5] If anything, it is in its interest to dissipate the revenues it receives from its special privileges by using resources inefficiently or paying higher than competitive rates for resources, much the most important of which is labor.

There is little doubt that the Postal Service employs resources inefficiently. For instance, the use of third- and fourth-class post offices, which contribute less than 2 percent of receipts but account for 6 percent of labor costs, cannot be justified on economic criteria.[6] First-class post offices, which are only 13 percent of the total number, account for 90 percent of revenue and 85 percent of labor costs. Two-thirds of all post offices and branches produce an average annual revenue less than $8,000. Most of these could be closed without causing any deterioration in collection and delivery schedules. A recent Postal Service study concludes that 17,000 of the nation's 30,000 post offices, all in small towns, could be closed saving $490 million a year with no diminution of service. However, an uneconomic post office is not closed unless its postmaster retires, resigns, moves, or dies. In 1976 Congress added a number of other barriers to closure.[7] In the six years after the postal system was reorganized in an effort to improve its efficiency, the number of post offices decreased by only 3 percent (see

[5] A contingency fund of $537 million was authorized in a recent postal-rate case. See U.S. Postal Rate Commission, *Opinion and Recommended Decision: Postal Rate and Fee Increases*, Docket No. R76-1 (1975), p. 51.

[6] See Table 2 for a breakdown of the number of post offices and branches between 1970-1975.

[7] See Walter S. Mossberg, *Wall Street Journal*, May 9, 1977, p. 11. Also see P.L. 94-421, section 2(e)ff.

Table 2

POSTAL SERVICE OFFICES, STATIONS, AND BRANCHES,
FISCAL YEARS ENDING JUNE 30

	1975	1974	1973	1972	1971	1970
Number of post offices	30,754	31,000	31,385	31,686	31,947	32,002
Number of branches and stations						
Classified branches and stations	3,993	3,955	3,939	3,729	3,906	3,869
Contract branches and stations	3,808	3,952	4,096	4,603	4,437	4,963
Community post offices	1,991	2,007	2,014	2,236	1,997	2,278
Total	9,792	9,914	10,049	10,568	10,340	11,110
Grand total	40,546	40,914	41,434	42,254	42,287	43,112

Source: *Annual Report of the Postmaster General, 1973-1974*, p. 51; *1974-1975*, p. 53.

Table 2). Uneconomic offices are retained largely to maintain a federal presence in the nation's small towns.[8]

The larger first-class post offices in typical downtown locations incur higher real estate costs than would be required if they were located elsewhere. These higher costs are only partially offset by the benefits of having facilities well situated to handle the large portion of mail that originates and is delivered to downtown locations. Since reorganization, the Postal Service has been attempting, in the face of strong union opposition, to put its major facilities in less congested areas in order to facilitate truck transportation.

The costs of constructing new postal facilities are also high. In 1967, they varied from seventeen dollars to thirty-six dollars per square foot, depending primarily on location of the facility, whereas general industry paid only eight dollars to twenty dollars per square foot for comparable space.[9]

Before reorganization capital expenditures were determined by the Congress. In those years many capital projects with ample expectation of substantial financial return remained incomplete. Equipment developed and used for one specific function or locality was not used in or adapted for related areas elsewhere.[10] An example is the multiposition letter sorter, a machine that requires ten fewer employees to sort a given amount of mail than conventional sorting techniques and is supposed to pay for itself in two years or less in a normal installation. The first of these was installed in a post office in 1959. By 1967, the equipment was used in only 39 post offices, by 1974 in only 176—and even where it was used it was not used to fullest advantage.[11]

Since reorganization, much more has been committed and spent for capital improvements, as can be seen in Table 3. Since postal reorganization in 1971, capital investment for new facilities, equipment, and vehicles has amounted to $3.2 billion; an almost threefold increase over the previous five-year period. But even with this the Postal Service has less than $1,500 in capital investment per employee while

---

[8] "The Postal Service has an immense national value . . . as the presence of the United States Government in cities, towns and villages throughout the land." U.S. Postal Service Board of Governors, *The Private Express Statutes and Their Administration*, Kappel Commission, 1973, Washington, D.C., p. 8.

[9] Kappel Commission, *Towards Postal Excellence*, vol. 1, p. 51.

[10] Ibid., p. 175.

[11] Charles E. McBride and Robert H. Cohen, "Sorting Mechanization Requirements in Large, Medium and Small Post Offices" (unpublished manuscript, annotated copy of slides), U.S. Postal Service Mail Classification Research Division, 1974.

Table 3

CAPITAL INVESTMENTS
BEFORE AND AFTER REORGANIZATION

Fiscal Year	Capital Investments ($ millions)
1966	$111.3
1967	148.7
1968	225.7
1969	235.5
1970	248.3
1971	235.4
1972	725.2
1973	805.9
1974	463.9
1975	735.1

Source: *Annual Report of the Postmaster General, 1974-1975,* p. 14.

capital investment per employee in office work is $2,000; in manufacturing, $25,000; in agriculture, $35,000; and in public utilities, nearly $70,000. A special unit under Carl C. Ulsaker, the senior assistant postmaster general for manpower and cost control, has used decentralized budgets to try to instill incentives for implementing cost-saving techniques. (In several cases this backfired as regional managers falsified mail volume figures to appear more efficient.) In practice the Postal Service has not been able to reduce the number of its employees by mechanization.

Advanced equipment like the multiposition letter sorters, parcel sorters, sack sorters, and cullers are limited to large post offices. Where used they have resulted in more than a proportionate increase in errors, with the result that more and more manpower is needed to handle a growing mail volume.[12] Since there is no reward for producing "surpluses," there is no incentive actually to decrease the number of jobs and thereby labor costs.[13] The economies of scale claimed by some to justify the service's legal monopoly simply do not exist.

Given augmented revenues and no profit incentive, it would not be surprising to find both operating inefficiencies and excessive wages

---

[12] Kappel Commission, *Towards Postal Excellence,* vol. 5, Summary, p. 27.

[13] Many people believe that the training and motivation of supervisors is critical for postal efficiency since they control labor utilization and productivity. Ibid., vol. 1, p. 65.

using up Postal Service revenues. The purpose of this study is to ascertain whether, and to what extent (if any), excessive wages have been paid to Postal Service employees.

Has Reorganization Solved the Incentive Problem?

The Postal Reorganization Act of 1970 introduced changes in the way the U.S. Post Office operated, the way postal rates were established, and the position of the Postal Service within the structure of the executive branch. The act abolished the Post Office Department and created a quasi-independent establishment within the executive branch of the government, called the U.S. Postal Service, to own and operate the nation's postal system. The Postal Service is directed by an eleven-man board of governors, nine of whom are appointed by the President to represent the public interest. The other two members are the postmaster general and the deputy postmaster general. The act established an independent Postal Rate Commission composed of five commissioners appointed by the President. The rate commission holds hearings on rate requests by the board of governors, then "recommends" reasonable and equitable rates for classes of mail and fees for postal services.

Another major feature of the act required that the Postal Service pay wages comparable to those paid for similar work in other sectors. There was, however, no mechanism established to determine when comparable wage levels were reached. Postmaster General Bailar recently stated that, in his opinion, postal wages had caught up with those paid elsewhere for similar work and that management would take this into account in bargaining.[14]

Do these organizational changes provide the incentives for management to pay competitive wages to its employees? The reorganization was accompanied by a pay increase of 14 percent, plus a shortening of the time required to attain step increases based on length of service. Subsequent bargaining has yielded the Postal Service employees wage increases greater than the average for all manufacturing firms. For instance, the collective bargaining agreement for July 21, 1973, to July 20, 1975, provided for a $700 a year pay increase effective July 21, 1973, and another $400 a year increase effective July 21, 1974. There were also four cost-of-living pay adjustments during the two-year period. In addition, the Postal Service twice increased its share of

---

[14] "Why Postal Rates Will Go Up Again: Interview with Benjamin F. Bailar, Postmaster General," *U.S. News and World Report*, March 17, 1975, p. 31.

the premium payments for health and medical insurance. In the second year of the contract it paid the entire premium for basic life insurance. The new contract signed September 1975 covering three years adds an average 4.2 percent a year increase in wages and benefits, plus semiannual cost-of-living adjustments. During fiscal years 1974, 1975, and 1976, when the consumer price index increased a total of 29 percent over fiscal year 1973, cost-of-living allowances produced compensation increases of $2.9 billion.

The pay increases for postal employees as compared with those in most industries for the same period gives little support for the view that the reorganization has somehow motivated postal management to pay its workers competitive wages. Postmaster Bailar would not even pretend to have done this. He said, "Postal workers have done well in the last six or eight years. I think their gains have exceeded those in the consumer price index. It is my understanding that one of the intentions of the original Postal Reorganization Act was to improve the level of wages in the Postal Service."[15] In 1970, hourly earnings of nonsupervisory postal employees, exclusive of fringe benefits, exceeded those of private nonfarm, nonsupervisory employees by 25 percent. By 1975, the excess in the pay rate of postal employees had grown to 35 percent. This evidence alone, however, does not demonstrate whether or not postal employees are overpaid. At this point, whether postal pay rates remain excessive is conjecture. We will examine the empirical evidence in chapter 4 before drawing any conclusions about the appropriateness of the level of wages paid to Postal Service employees.

Postal Deficits

Each year the Postal Service suffers a large financial deficit. This was not always so. Before the 1840s, the system reported only budgetary surpluses, and in the sixty-nine years between 1850 and 1919 it reported surpluses in twelve years. Since 1919 the system has operated at a deficit every year except for the war years 1943-1945.[16]

With rare exceptions, postal rate legislation has been prompted by recurring postal deficits, and since 1945 all rate increases have been designed to eliminate increases in that deficit. The Postal Policy Act

[15] See U.S., Congress, House of Representatives, Committee on the Post Office and Civil Service, Subcommittee on Postal Operations and Service, *Proceedings, Hearing on Oversight of the United States Postal Service*, 95th Congress, 1st session, March 15, 1977, p. 29.

[16] Kappel Commission, *Towards Postal Excellence*, vol. 2, pp. 2-6.

of 1958 suggested that postal expenditures should be covered by revenues from services plus congressional appropriations called "public service" subsidies.[17] The act also sought to sharpen the distinction between losses arising from mail carried at regular rates and those arising from "public service" functions by identifying the specific public services involved. The list of public services was expanded in 1962 and the method of measuring their costs was changed in 1967. In fiscal 1967, public service costs amounted to $567 million, or nearly one-half of the total deficit.[18]

The essence of the 1958 act was that public service operations were to be financed by taxpayers, and all other operations were to be financed by the users without requiring that each class of mail be self-supporting.[19] What happened was that despite the growing proportion of postal operations labeled "public services," other operations did not become self-supporting. Indeed, postal deficits, even with the contribution from public services excluded have continued to mount.

The Post Office Department was insulated from any need to worry about funds. Congress established the basis for most costs, handed out subsidies, and provided supplemental appropriations to cover losses. Under the reorganization, the Postal Service is supposed to cover more of its costs and the subsidy is to be gradually phased out. As Figure 1 shows, there is no indication of progress in this direction. In 1977 the federal subsidy calculated as a fixed charge for postal service amounts to approximately three dollars per household per month.

The Postal Service has the authority to borrow money and issue bonds up to a total obligation of $10 billion at any one time, and it may use this source of funds to cover its costs. However, congressional help is provided in the form of an annual subsidy whose size is set at (1) 10 percent of the Post Office Department's total 1971 appropriation, plus (2) an amount determined by the Postal Service as required to cover the costs of mail sent free or at reduced costs, and (3) an additional amount to aid in the transition to the Postal Service. Beginning with fiscal 1972, the first component of the subsidy has amounted to $920 million a year (10 percent of the Post Office's fiscal 1971 appropriation), and the other components have varied between $0.5 and $1.1 billion dollars a year. The first component is supposed to be reduced gradually after 1979, until it reaches 5 percent of the

---

17 Ibid., pp. 2-3.
18 Ibid., pp. 2-8.
19 Ibid., pp. 2-3.

Figure 1

POSTAL OPERATING INCOME AND EXPENSE

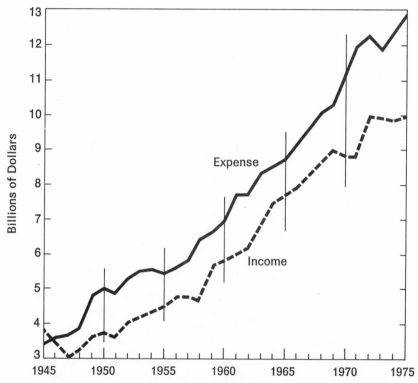

Source: Donald R. Ewing and Roger K. Salaman, *The Postal Crisis: The Postal Function as a Communications Service* (Washington, D.C.: U.S. Department of Commerce, Office of Telecommunications, January 1977), p. 2.

1971 appropriation ($460 million) by 1984, and it may be dropped altogether after that. If this plan is followed, an increasing portion of Postal Service revenues will come from its customers.[20]

Postage Rate Setting in the Postal Service

Operating revenues of the Postal Service come primarily from postage fees charged for carrying of the mails and, to a limited extent, from special services. Before reorganization, it was necessary for the President and the Bureau of the Budget (BOB) to approve the Post Office's

---

[20] "Postal Service at One Year: Still a Long Way to Go," *National Report* (Washington, D.C.: Congressional Quarterly, Inc., 1972), p. 1275.

request for new rates before a rate increase bill could be submitted to Congress. The only BOB personnel working on postal affairs consisted of two, and at times three, full-time analysts and a half-time assistant chief. Its main concerns were the total size of the Post Office Department budget, subsequent apportionment of the approved appropriations, and especially the elimination of the deficit. It had relatively little interest in the structure of rates. For its part, the department, though not indifferent to postal deficits, did upon occasion resist the full extent of the revenue increases sought by the Budget Bureau.

Getting a rate bill through Congress began with informal negotiations with key members to try to anticipate congressional desires and to determine optimum timing, after which identical bills were usually transmitted simultaneously to the House and Senate. Rate setting was a political issue involving the Congress, the President, and the Bureau of the Budget, with organized groups actively resisting increases affecting themselves. Political and personal conflicts within and between the two houses contributed to delays. Attempts to reconcile these interests sometimes dragged out rate setting for two years or more.[21]

The 1958 Postal Policy Act was an attempt to state clear criteria that would permit rate making at the congressional committee level, but it was unsuccessful. Rather than establishing rates on the basis of stated criteria, the House and Senate committees on postal matters alternated between a vague concern for the "public services" performed by the Post Office, which mitigated against rate increases, and a search for a formula that would end controversy among the vested interests and facilitate an equitable upward adjustment of rates. Testimony by Post Office officials on cost data or their desire to offer the best possible service with their scarce resources was considered irrelevant. Members of Congress referred to public service as their criteria, connoting benefit to the whole community and operation on a "nonprofit" basis without concern for efficiency. The result of this process was to satisfy as many pressure groups as possible, not to charge postal patrons for mail services provided.

In congressional committee hearings, Post Office officials usually testified first, defending the rate bill and generally arguing that the differentials between classes of mail should be narrowed. Next, interested parties representing second- and third-class mailers testified. Their presentations were characterized by self-interest, justified by public benefits, with no reference to cost criteria. Testimony by or in

---

[21] Kappel Commission, *Towards Postal Excellence*, vol. 1, p. 113.

behalf of first-class users was rare. Most witnesses either advocated increases in only first-class mail rates or set forth reasons why classes other than their own should bear a relatively greater share of the burden. Only a few supported proportionate increases in the rates on all classes of mail. Second- and third-class users were relatively successful in resisting a narrowing of the differential with first-class mail.[22]

Political practicalities and expediency reduced the department's influence on rate making to mere anticipation of congressional desire. It is not surprising that Post Office officials wished to remove discussions of rates from an open process, in which contending interests were reconciled, to an agency or authority independent of those interests, where their own expert views would be more influential and the delays in securing rate legislation would be shortened.

The reorganization bill of the administration proposed that the Postal Rate Commission be an advisory board within the Postal Service, a board that could not only grant rate changes but also watch expenditures. However, the House-Senate conference committee made the board independent of the Postal Service. The Postal Service has the power to set temporary rates while the Postal Rate Commission weighs permanent rates. As an independent commission the latter has no jurisdiction over Postal Service expenditures. The Postal Service estimates the revenues it needs over and above its income from current rates and appropriations. The commission is then obliged to increase the rates on the various classes of mail to raise the estimated additional revenue. In this vacuum of accountability, the Postal Service determines its "needs" and then turns to Congress and the Postal Rate Commission for its revenue.

Since the reorganization, postal rate increases have been instituted with considerably more ease than they were before. The August 1973 increase in postal rates was the second of five annual increments for second-, third-, and fourth-class, and controlled-circulation mail recommended in 1972 by the Postal Rate Commission.[23] Magazine publishers contended this would be disastrous for their publications. The new rates set out in a complicated Postal Service schedule varied according to weight and destination as well as by class of mail. For example, postage costs for a typical second-class weekly publication

---

[22] Ibid., vol. 2, pp. 8-9.

[23] Those interested in the postage rate schedule for the different classifications of mail should consult, U.S. Postal Rate Commission, *Opinion and Recommended Decision: Postal Rate and Fee Increases*, Docket No. R71-1 (June 5, 1972), Appendix 2.

mailed within the same county, such as a small-town newspaper, increased from 0.6 to 0.7 of a cent for each copy. The rate for nationally distributed periodicals of nonprofit organizations rose from 0.75 to 0.9 of a cent per copy. The second-class rate for a typical commercial periodical, such as *Time* and *Newsweek*, went up from 2.8 to 3.4 cents a copy. Third-class bulk mail rates for the booklets often distributed by nonprofit organizations increased from 8 cents to 9 cents per pound. Fourth-class rates applied to books and records went up from 14 to 16 cents for the first pound and from 7 to 8 cents for additional pounds.[24]

Since reorganization some mail users have protested to Congress because of the large increases in their rates. In 1974 Congress passed a law increasing the period for the annual phased increase of rates from five to eight years for some commercial users and from ten to sixteen years for nonprofit institutions. After major rate cases initiated in 1974 and 1976, the Postal Rate Commission has approved two more across-the-board rate increases for the Postal Service. Another rate case is expected that will probably raise rates again in 1978, after a congressional moratorium on rate increases expires in late 1977. The Postal Service is expected to argue that it needs the increases to offset its usual deficit, which, some predict, may be around $1 billion.[25]

The increased facility in raising postal rates since reorganization makes it easier for the Postal Service to exploit its monopoly position and maximize its revenues. These increased revenues become available to the Postal Service to pay for increases in wage costs.

---

[24] Margaret Gentry, "Rise Allowed in Mail Rates," *Washington Post*, September 1, 1973.

[25] "Additional income—from some source—will . . . be needed in 1978. . . . We may formally apply for an increase in the next few months." Speech by Postmaster General Bailar before the Comstock Club, Sacramento, California, February 7, 1977.

2

PERSONNEL ADMINISTRATION IN THE POSTAL SERVICE

A faithful employee is as refreshing
as a cool day in the hot summertime.
Proverbs 25:13

This chapter examines how the Postal Service chooses its top managers, how they supervise postal affairs, and how the constraints and incentives within the system affect managers and workers. The last area of inquiry is particularly important for understanding the efficiency, or lack of efficiency, in postal operations—throughout the history of the Post Office as well as since reorganization. The object is to ascertain whether, to what extent, and possibly why, excessive wages were paid to postal employees not only after but also before reorganization. The internal operations of the Postal Service are categorized and described to determine the amount of education, training, and technical skill needed to perform most job functions. This information provides an intuitive basis for assessing the skill required of postal workers, which in turn helps assess the level of wages necessary to attract the postal work force.

Consideration is also given to how employees are treated, to the level of their nonpecuniary benefits, and to the security of their jobs. These factors naturally enhance the attractiveness of postal employment and have real value to employees. Union operations are examined in some detail and, finally, the wage schedule and its classifications are addressed. This chapter provides institutional information helpful to understanding the wage determination process in the Postal Service.

Management and the Postal Complex

Before reorganization the President appointed the postmaster general and other top managers, with the advice and consent of the Senate, for the length of his own term plus one month. These appointments tended to be political. Some postmasters general were so close to the President that political duties overshadowed postal duties. In these situations the Post Office was without effective leadership.

The postmaster general's power was severely limited by rules and practices determined in the "postal complex" and was substantially out of his control. The postal complex included all those agencies of the federal government performing functions that would have been handled by the Post Office had it been a business enterprise. The most important element in the postal complex was Congress. There was almost no limit to the areas of postal management in which Congress became involved. It passed laws, conducted formal hearings, and indirectly appointed top management personnel (through patronage). Committee staff members collected information, followed up congressional requests, scheduled hearings and testimony, and provided communications between committees and the Post Office. At any time, Congress could change the rules of the union-management relationship, alter the relationships with the major mailers through rate and mailability provisions, and give postal officers more or less freedom to draw contracts with airlines, railroads, and building contractors.[1] It could require more or less public service. With these decisions Congress determined the policy of the Post Office.

Committees of the House and Senate were concerned with such employment conditions as wages, working conditions, fringe benefits, job descriptions, duties, hours, and staffing levels. Postal appropriations were considered by the subcommittees on Treasury, Post Office, and Civil Service in both the House and the Senate. The Senate often acted as a counterbalance to the House by restoring cuts in appropriations made by the House. In addition, the Subcommittee on Deficiencies and Supplementals acted on postal requests for supplemental appropriations. The membership of the Post Office and Civil Service Committee did not overlap with Appropriations; therefore responsibility for costs was separated from responsibility for providing funds. All budget requests were defended before a subcommittee of the Appropriations Committee. Compensation of all government employees,

---

[1] The postmaster general had authority to make rules and regulations for the carriage of the mail by aircraft consistent with the provisions of the Federal Aviation Act or any rule or regulation made by the Civil Aeronautics Board.

including postal workers, was determined by a subcommittee of the Post Office and Civil Service Committee.

In addition to Congress, the postal complex included such regulatory agencies as the Civil Service Commission, the Civil Aeronautics Board, the General Services Administration, and the Interstate Commerce Commission, each of which had a special interest in and some control over activities of the Post Office. These agencies influenced policy and operations in the areas of their own interest. For instance, the Civil Service Commission exercised control over personnel regulations for examinations, hiring, employment, supervision, and discipline of employees. Through these regulations, not necessarily designed for postal employees, the Civil Service Commission preempted much of the personnel administration of the Post Office. The Civil Aeronautics Board was empowered to fix fair and reasonable air freight rates, to prescribe methods of ascertaining compensation, and to publish rules pertaining to the transport of airmail. The General Services Administration provided the Post Office with a management system for its property and records. The Interstate Commerce Commission (ICC) had authority to fix rates for railway transportation of mail. Rates on fourth-class mail could not be changed without ICC approval. While the ICC could not require the Post Office to use railway cars, it could influence this decision.

Given this dissipation of decision-making power among agencies outside the Post Office, it is not surprising that the Post Office was not managed like a nationwide system. An average of 2,200 postmasters reported to each of the fifteen regional directors, and there was little opportunity for real communication and direction. The result was that the Post Office was operated as an aggregation of semi-autonomous post offices held together by the postal manual, regional instructions, assorted directives, and a common source of funds.

The Kappel Commission saw the principal failure of the Post Office as one of management. It concluded that productivity could be increased substantially if supervisors were better trained, motivated, and rewarded. Managers are in fact critical to overall efficiency, since they control labor utilization. If a private company had the sort of shortcomings the Post Office had in service, working conditions, and pricing policy, a new management team would be installed. While the Kappel Commission believed that a reorganized Postal Service would correct the most important efficiency problems, its hopes have not been realized.

From the Post Office's point of view, the close congressional control of all operations, and especially personnel matters, was an impediment, and the interference from the regulatory agencies was a nuisance. Reorganization removed many of these hindrances to Post Office control but did not structure the incentive system to make the pursuit of efficiency coincident with the welfare of the managers and employees. Consequently, reorganization did not provide an incentive for the Postal Service to pay its employees competitive wages.

Internal Operations of the Postal Service

The Postal Service's basic function is the processing of mail, which includes cards, envelopes, newspapers, magazines, catalogues, and parcels. Raw mail is collected, then separated into airmail, mail suitable for machine processing, and items of unusual size or shape which must be handled manually. Machinable mail is fed through a complicated device that faces it and cancels the stamps. It is then placed in trays for internal distribution to sorting clerks at manual cases or at letter-sorting machines. Local mail is sorted by carrier routes for delivery the next day. Mail leaving the city is sorted into canvas sacks, transported by truck, plane, train, or boat to its destination post office, and then sorted for delivery.[2] Not all mail passes through each stage of this process. For example, second-class publishers' mail is often privately hauled to the city in which it is to be distributed, and letters addressed to boxholders do not require delivery.

Revenue is collected for stamps, parcel post, and special services by window clerks. Collections are also made at post offices or at the mailer's premises for permit mail. There are a host of support functions such as industrial management, research and development, accounting and finance controls, and general management which do not ordinarily involve the handling of mail but are concerned with the direction and control of the whole process.

In fiscal year 1967, delivery service accounted for about 41 percent of total Post Office costs. This category includes preparation for delivery, delivery at post offices (putting mail into boxes or into general delivery) as well as to businesses and residences, parcel post delivery, rural and special delivery, and miscellaneous delivery service. Processing of mail in post offices accounted for about 33 percent of total mail costs. This category includes mail preparation, culling, facing, and cancelling outgoing and incoming distribution. Transpor-

---

[2] George M. Wattles, "Rates and Costs of the U.S. Postal Service," *Journal of Law and Economics*, vol. 16 (April 1973), p. 91.

tation, which is mostly purchased, accounted for about 15 percent of total postal costs. Direct services to mailers (which include all costs of window collection and automatic dispensing) accounted for about 6 percent of postal costs. All other postal activities, that is, law enforcement, research and development, general management, and auxiliary services accounted for about 5 percent of total costs. The percentages in this cost categorization have been relatively constant over time.

A post office's operating schedule centers on two daily peak loads—one in the morning for incoming mail and one in the evening for outgoing mail. The processing for the two periods is slightly different. Mail in the evening peak can generally be zip-sorted and then scheduled according to a transportation scheme, but the morning load must be sorted according to carrier routes, which requires a knowledge of "schemes," or distribution patterns. To accommodate the peaks in the workload, the twenty-four hour workday is divided into three tours. Tour one from 12:00 midnight to 8:00 a.m. is devoted to incoming mail; tour two from 8:00 a.m. to 4:00 p.m. is devoted primarily to accelerated business collection, delivery of mail, and processing low-priority mail; and tour three from 4:00 p.m. to 12:00 midnight is devoted to outgoing mail. The shifts from 4:00 a.m. to 12:00 noon, 6:00 a.m. to 2:00 p.m., and 7:00 a.m. to 3:00 p.m. overlap tours one and two; shifts from 9:00 a.m. to 5:00 p.m. and 12:00 noon to 10:00 p.m. overlap tours two and three. Tour three is the busiest, with the greatest volume fluctuation and overlapping work assignments. Tour two generally is the least pressed, but employs the most experienced workers who, by virtue of their seniority, have elected daytime work. Employees are assigned to each tour as manpower needs require.

Local postal officials have only limited control over the number of positions available to them. A post office does not set its own workload; the load is set by the public since the post office cannot refuse to handle legitimate mail. Given the workload, staffing needs are determined by set criteria, size of the installation, and postal volume. The postmaster is responsible for man-hours rather than people or dollars and cannot create positions that exceed his clerical complement. For instance, if average sorting productivity is 1,200 pieces per hour, one clerk could be added for every additional 1,200 pieces per hour received, as long as the postmaster remained within his assigned complement. Daily work-hour reports submitted by the postmaster to the data center show departures from estimates and help determine manpower increases or decreases. For periods of less than one week, labor is scheduled by the superintendent of mails in the individual post office. The regional office establishes a general framework within which the superintendent operates, but the variations in workload necessitate adjustments on both a daily and a tour basis.

Types of Postal Employees

In matching manpower with workloads, postal officials can draw on four principal categories of employees: career regulars, hourly rate regulars, career substitutes, and temporary substitutes. Career regulars include postmasters, supervisors, and rural carriers as well as most clerks, carriers, and mail handlers. These permanent full-time employees make up about 70 percent of postal employees. They are salaried, so their earnings are unaffected by the number of hours worked (unless overtime is involved), and they cannot be discharged except "for cause," so they enjoy almost continuous tenure. Once assigned to a post office, a career regular may not be transferred against his or her will. Hourly rate regulars are permanent part-time employees with fixed work schedules usually not exceeding twenty hours a week. Career substitutes have no fixed schedule and are used to augment the regular work force during peak periods. The hourly rate regulars and the career substitutes make up about 15 percent of postal employees. Temporary employees account for the last 15 percent of the work force. They are hired to replace those on summer vacation or to meet the Christmas rush. In staffing a post office, priority must be given to career regulars; substitutes can be used in the ratio of one to every five career regulars, and hourly rate regulars can be employed only when no more flexibility is obtainable by using regulars and substitutes. In addition, officials cannot hire more temporary seasonal employees than the number of employees hired within the preceding ninety-day period.

Postal Occupations

From Table 4 it can be seen that, except for inspectors and managers reporting to headquarters, the occupational composition of the postal work force changed little between 1970 and 1975. There is no evidence in this period that mechanization had a significant impact upon the composition of the postal labor force, in terms of either increased demands for more skilled personnel or decreased demands for those occupations most likely to be affected by mechanization, such as clerks. The diffusion of existing mechanical devices and the introduc-

24

Table 4

PERCENTAGE DISTRIBUTION OF THE POSTAL LABOR FORCE BY OCCUPATION, 1970-1975
(on payroll as of June 30)

Employee Groups	1975	1974	1973	1972	1971	1970
Headquarters employees	00.4	00.4	00.4	00.3	00.4	00.4
Field regular employees:						
Regional and other field units reporting to headquarters	01.9	01.4	00.7	00.8	00.8	00.9
Inspection service	00.7	00.7	00.7	00.7	00.3	00.3
Postmasters	04.3	04.3	04.2	04.4	04.1	04.0
Post office supervisors and technical personnel	05.3	05.3	04.9	05.4	05.1	05.0
Post office clerks and mail handlers	34.0	34.2	34.1	35.4	32.9	32.8
City delivery carriers and vehicle drivers	23.8	24.1	24.5	24.8	22.8	22.3
Rural delivery carriers	04.4	04.3	04.3	04.3	04.3	04.2
Special delivery messengers	00.4	00.4	00.4	00.5	00.4	00.4
Building and equipment maintenance personnel	03.6	03.5	03.4	03.4	03.1	03.0
Vehicle maintenance facility personnel	00.7	00.7	00.8	00.8	00.8	00.7
Total regular employees	79.6	79.5	78.3	80.8	74.9	74.0
Total substitute employees	20.4	20.5	21.7	19.2	25.1	26.0
Total	100.0	100.0	100.0	100.0	100.0	100.0

Source: *Annual Report of the Postmaster General, 1973-1974,* p. 51.

tion of new equipment should have increased the demand for highly skilled personnel, but did not. Since the pace of mechanization is not expected to increase in the future, the occupational composition of the postal labor force is unlikely to change significantly in the near future.

Clerks and mail handlers make up about 34 percent of the Postal Service labor force. The distribution clerks, who must possess "scheme" knowledge (that is, a large number of destination and distribution points committed to memory), separate incoming or outgoing mail in a post office terminal, airmail field, or other postal facility, sorting the mail by machine or by hand. These clerks are required to take a state scheme examination covering every post office, station, and branch listed in the scheme. A city scheme examination requires similar knowledge of the local scheme. A grade of 95 percent must be obtained to pass. Window clerks perform a variety of services at a public window of a post office, branch, or station. As representatives of the Postal Service, clerks are to be familiar with postal laws, regulations, and procedures and to maintain pleasant and effective public relations with patrons. Mail handlers load, unload, and move bulk mail; perform sorting duties not requiring scheme knowledge; and operate certain mail-processing machines.

City and rural letter carriers, who constitute about 29 percent of the total work force, sort mail for their own delivery. They receive less supervision than the clerks because most of their work is performed individually outdoors. Rural carriers, in addition to delivering mail, provide "retail" postal services such as selling stamps and receiving parcels. Their compensation is based on route length, patrons served, and mail volume. Their workday ends when they complete their deliveries and a few clerical duties. Before reorganization, rural carriers and postmasters were the only postal employees who were formally appointed through the political process with an imposed residence requirement.[3] Independent contractors called star-route carriers deliver mail in remote areas where other service cannot be provided easily.

Maintenance employees' duties range from operating elevators and serving as janitors to repairing automotive, air conditioning, and mail-processing equipment. Motor vehicle employees pick up and transport mail by truck on regularly scheduled routes. Special delivery messengers deliver all classes of special delivery mail, usually by vehicle. These groups make up about 5 percent of the postal labor force.

Each occupation is strictly regulated by a job description supple-

---

[3] Kappel Commission, *Towards Postal Excellence*, vol. 5, p. 103.

mented by manuals and letters of instruction that detail the nature of the work and the manner of performing it. The employee is responsible for performing a minutely described, routine job. The technology is basically simple, notwithstanding the increased use of machines in some phases of the operation. Except for a relatively small number of jobs, mainly maintenance positions requiring mechanical or technical skills and perhaps some scheme jobs, the occupational requirements in postal crafts are not exacting. The most stringent regulations affecting the largest number of employees are the proficiency requirements for the distribution and dispatching of mail by scheme clerks.

Postal Personnel Functions

Because the Postal Service is labor-intensive, it depends primarily on employees' performance in individual and group tasks, rather than on machine performance. Hiring, training, supervising, promoting, and directing a large dispersed body of employees is an extensive and complex undertaking not unlike that of the army, where functions and procedures are stated, rules apply, and authority is delegated. Higher officials receive documents from their superiors that expand on their job descriptions and become the basis for further subdivisions of responsibilities to permit the assignment of tasks to subordinates. It is the responsibility of each person to relate any particular situation to the existing regulatory framework—the general rule in government being that nothing can be done unless there is specific authority for doing it. Tasks are so highly subdivided that no one carries out what could be called a complete unit of work.[4]

Routine employees occupy standardized positions governed by general instructions recorded in the postal manual.[5] This manual defines relationships, procedures, and attitudes and confers authority to organizational units to perform the duties and responsibilities assigned to them.[6] It is intended to be a self-contained guide covering all foreseeable contingencies for all decisions to be made regarding the administration of postal affairs.[7] With few changes from the Post

---

[4] Ibid., vol. 3, p. 3.8.

[5] "Each installation head makes the Postal Service Manual available to all employees. When there is no personnel office the availability and location of a reference copy of the Postal Manual is posted on employee bulletin boards. Supervisors and personnel officers counsel and advise employees on the meaning of the various sections of the manual." See "General Transmittal Letter 1," in U.S. Postal Service, *Postal Service Manual*, chapter 6.

[6] Kappel Commission, *Towards Postal Excellence*, vol. 3, p. 3.10.

[7] Ibid., vol. 1, p. 45.

Office days it has remained the handbook for postal employees since reorganization. In a word, the Postal Service goes by the book.

The Postal Service organization is designed to be directed from the top rather than to be responsive to changes from below. One has only to memorize the postal manual to be a satisfactory Postal Service employee. Any deviation ordered verbally must be confirmed by a written memorandum or order, and postal inspectors are directed to charge as "irregularities" any deviations not properly authorized. One goes by the rules or is punished. Except in emergencies such as fires or floods, no deviations from the postal manual are permitted. This comprehensive book of rules makes it easy for individual managers and supervisors, in their interactions with subordinates, to avoid personal responsibility for their actions by placing the blame on the directives.

The postal manual states: "Any communication on matters requiring discretion or policy determinations shall proceed through each successive level of authority upward and downward without bypassing any." This practice is followed to give an officer who is accountable for any activity the opportunity to pass judgment on matters under his jurisdiction. Since irregularities uncovered by the postal inspectors can have serious consequences for the local manager or supervisor, employees' initiatives are fraught with risk. Irregularities are easy enough to uncover because it is beyond the capability of any single individual to know all the rules. Many in the organization can recall instances when such irregularities were used to fire postmasters or to block promotions. The lesson is "don't stick your neck out, don't rock the boat, don't make waves." The safest course is to stick to the book or pass responsibility up the line.

The service enforces postal laws through its inspection service of picked and trained personnel. The inspectors devote about half their time to mail theft, mail fraud, obscenity, and other postal crimes and half to management functions such as inspection, audit, special studies, and investigations. Their job is to uncover and examine irregularities in the implementation of regulations. If they find an employee who has committed a mail crime, they make a citizen's arrest and present the offender to a U.S. attorney who prepares the complaint.

An employee found guilty of an irregularity may be subjected to an adverse action which can result in suspension, discharge from employment, furlough without pay, or reduction in rank or compensation. These are quite properly called "pocketbook" issues. Adverse action procedures were imposed on departments and agencies on

January 17, 1962, by Executive Order 10988. If the employee does not agree with the proposed action, he may make a reply to the responsible official in the Postal Service hierarchy. If the employee is unable to receive satisfaction, he may pursue the action within the Postal Service to the regional level or he may appeal to the Civil Service Commission after receipt of the notice of the adverse decision. If he chooses the departmental route, his next stage is a decision by the appropriate regional executive.

After a decision at the regional level of the service, the employee still has three options: he can go to the Postal Service's Board of Appeals and Review, he can go to the Civil Service Commission, or he can, with the concurrence of his union, request advisory arbitration. Almost all employees involved in adverse actions take the departmental route. Apparently employees feel confident of a fair hearing on the merits of the case within the department or, since 1971, the Postal Service. The Civil Service Commission will only reverse a decision on procedural violations, and reportedly does not usually accept claims of mitigating circumstances. Employees feel that the Civil Service Commission gives the local postmaster the benefit of the doubt as far as substantive issues are concerned and hears appeals only for procedural violations.

Officials in local installations have complained about the length of time it takes to get rid of "incompetents" or "troublemakers." The process of preparing documents and appearing at conferences, meetings, and hearings discourages adverse actions by managers. An employee against whom a removal action is pending can stay on the active roll until the appeal is decided at the regional level, a process that takes sixty to ninety days. During this time the employee, if he or she expects to be dismissed, may disrupt the morale and discipline of the office. Fellow workers are generally unaware of the existence of the action because the supervisor cannot disclose it. When employees witness an apparently helpless supervisor repeatedly being challenged, discipline breaks down and may not be restored for a long time. Because of the difficulty in applying disciplinary actions, supervisors have only informal power over their subordinates. They are helped by the sense of commitment to "moving the mails" that prevails throughout the organization, but when this commitment is insufficient, they must coax or bluff employees to get the job done. When it proves necessary to take disciplinary action against an employee, the overriding requirement is that the action be corrective rather than punitive and be influenced by considerations of individual dignity, justice, and equality.[8] Disciplinary action is rarely used because the procedure is too intricate, long, and cumbersome.

Any issue or matter not defined in the national collective bargaining agreement between postal unions and management may be the subject for a grievance. Grievances fall into two categories: those based on racial or sexual discrimination, and all other types (covering such matters as work schedules, assignments, and mail distribution schemes). Grievances are handled at as low a level as possible, mainly by the local postmaster or supervising official. Before reorganization, discriminatory grievances were handled outside the department and could be appealed to the Civil Service Commission or to the Department of Labor.[9] If an employee used the grievance procedure up to the Appeal and Review Board in Washington, more than 105 calendar days could elapse during the process.

A new grievance system was set up in the reorganization whereby an employee deals directly with his immediate supervisor and the head of his installation. If they are unable to resolve the grievance, he may appeal to a hearing committee. If the grievance process is carried up to and through the regional director, assuming all parties act immediately, it takes a minimum of 140 calendar days. But it can easily take longer since there appears to be no stated time period within which an employee must appeal the supervisor's action and no limit to the time used for an informal hearing at the regional office.

Because of long delays in handling grievances, an expedited arbitration panel was assembled on January 1, 1974—on an experimental basis for a period of one year—to handle disciplinary cases not involving an interpretation of the agreement and not involving technical or policy-making issues. The unions and the Postal Service, with the aid of the American Arbitration Association, the Federal Mediation and Conciliation Service, deans of law schools, and the National Academy of Arbitrators—provided a list of arbitrators from which a designated arbitrator was chosen on a rotation system to conduct the hearing. The arbitrator's decision was intended to be final. This scheme did not work and is no longer in existence.

The Patronage System

Before the reorganization, eligibility for appointment to postmaster was contingent on residence within the office's delivery area, a requirement that limited the number of candidates and prevented the transfer

---

[8] "General Transmittal Letter 1," Postal Service Manual, part 443.

[9] Kappel Commission, Towards Postal Excellence, vol. 4, p. 7.55.

of successful postmasters to vacancies in larger cities. An "adviser" system controlled the appointment process. The adviser was usually a local congressman belonging to the political party in power nationally, or a majority party senator, governor, or state or county party chairman. When a vacancy occurred an acting postmaster was selected by the adviser. The adviser could recommend a career employee or elevate a clerk or carrier over the heads of better qualified employees. Once the adviser selected a candidate for permanent appointment, the Civil Service Commission conducted a character check and gave a competitive examination to determine the top three candidates. The examination could be repeated until the adviser's choice fell within the top three and so could be selected. During this period, the adviser could simply withhold advice, giving technical reasons to justify the holding of new examinations. Long delays could occur while the adviser waited for his favored candidate to qualify or for his newly hired "substitute" to be eligible for a noncompetitive appointment after ninety days.[10] In the period from 1958 to 1966 when this patronage system was in force, only a third of the 9,000 postmaster jobs filled were given to career service employees.[11]

Over the same period some 30,000 rural letter carriers who had met Civil Service qualifications were appointed by a similar patronage process. Once appointed they could exchange their rural routes for others anywhere in the country without meeting new residency requirements. In addition to other appealing aspects of their employment, rural carriers have a level of compensation well above the median income of their communities. Typically dozens and sometimes hundreds of applicants sought each rural carrier vacancy. The applicants frequently included postmasters, for whom such an appointment constituted a financial advantage.[12]

Political affiliation also entered into the appointment of other postal administrators, although to a lesser extent. Patronage in regional appointments, unlike that for postmasters and rural carriers, did not have a statutory basis and was managed informally. While political patronage was most important to members of Congress from rural areas, it was also important in many large urban areas where postal appointments were used to extend recognition to minority groups with growing political influence. In addition, there was an unspoken agreement among postmasters to promote the right people

---

[10] Ibid., vol. 5, p. 41.

[11] Ibid., p. 106.

[12] Ibid., p. 42.

politically to the supervisory and middle-management levels, even if merit had to be subordinated. Such an attitude was hardly conducive to good morale and career commitment.

The emphasis given to seniority and political acceptability in determining promotions created an environment in which employees were more concerned with job tenure and convenience than with performance. They could not earn promotions based on merit, so had little incentive to do more or better work. Those without the right political connection could not even aspire to leadership of their own post offices.

The patronage system limited the advancement opportunities of career employees with management potential and inevitably harmed morale. The postmaster selection process instituted since the 1970 reorganization has eliminated the patronage appointment. From postal reorganization until early 1977 impartial selection boards chose 15,500 new postmasters under the merit selection program.[13] However, there is now a rule that requires a postal employee to serve four or five years before becoming eligible for the supervisory examination. This prevents college graduates from moving directly into middle-management positions in the Postal Service and so reduces the prospects of substantially upgrading the quality and training of Postal Service supervisors.

Postal Union Strength and Activity

Before reorganization, Executive Order 10988 marked the beginning of formal labor-management relations in the federal government. That order, issued in 1962, directed federal agencies to recognize employee representatives for the purpose of negotiating agreements and to consult them on personnel matters.[14] Judging from the frequency and intensity of complaints on both sides, it has not been successful. In any event, until reorganization, the National Agreement between the seven bargaining unions and the Post Office was negotiated within the framework of Executive Order 10988. The stated aim of the agreement was to enhance the well-being of the employees and to maintain an efficient and economic operation.

The Postal Service is highly unionized. Between 70 and 90 per-

---

[13] *Comprehensive Statement of Postal Operations* presented to the Committees on Post Office and Civil Service and the Committees on Appropriations of the Senate and the House of Representatives pursuant to 39 U.S.C. 2401 (g), as added by P.L. No. 94-421, 1977, p. 28.

[14] Kappel Commission, *Towards Postal Excellence*, vol. 5, p. 19.

cent of postal employees belong to one or more of the employee organizations.[15] Precise percentages are difficult to ascertain. The number of employees in the unions engaged in negotiations with the Postal Service may differ from the number of members because some employees are represented only by a local union not recognized for national bargaining, because retired employees stay in the union for retirement benefits, and because some supervisors and postmasters remain members of employee organizations either for sentimental reasons or for the special benefits. Also, some unions have members who are not Postal Service employees, and these are not always separated in the membership figures. Columns 2, 3, and 4 of Table 5 show membership figures for postal unions in 1966-1967, 1968, and 1975. Since these organizations are not required to report their memberships, the figures are estimates. Union membership may have grown slightly faster than Postal Service employment since 1966-1967, since the union dues check-off has grown faster than employment.[16]

Some indication of union resources can be drawn from check-off data. In 1977, 88 percent of postal employees or approximately 615,000 postal union members authorized check-offs. The monthly contribution per member ranged from five dollars to eight dollars depending on the union, with an average of about seven dollars. Before the 1975 agreement the Post Office/Postal Service retained approximately 1 percent of the dues collected for administrative expenses. Beginning with the 1975 contract this expense was absorbed by the Postal Service. The unions receive approximately $4.3 million monthly from check-offs which amounts to about $50 million annually.[17]

Four unions listed in Table 5—the American Postal Workers Union, the National Association of Letter Carriers, the National Rural Letter Carriers Association, and the National Post Office Mail Handlers, Watchmen, Messengers and Group Leaders Division of Laborers' International Union of North America—exclusively represent postal workers at the national level. They encompass the bulk of the postal union membership and may also represent groups at local and

---

[15] *Postal Reform Proposals* (Washington, D.C.: American Enterprise Institute, 1970). Robert J. Meyers states in *The Coming Collapse of the Post Office*, (Englewood Cliffs, N.J.: Prentice-Hall, 1975), p. 26, that in 1975 over 80 percent of postal employees were union members.

[16] Between 1966-1967 and 1975 employment with the Post Office/Postal Service has declined from 713,771 to 702,257 for a decrease of 1.6 percent while the number of dues-paying union members has increased from 577,080 to 635,460 for an increase of 10.1 percent.

[17] The figures pertain to January 1977 and were obtained from union officials.

Table 5
POSTAL UNION STRENGTH

	Postal Employees Having Union Dues Deducted July 1967 (1)	Estimated Postal Union Membership		
		1966-1967 (2)	1968 (3)	1975 (4)
American Postal Workers Union, AFL-CIO				260,000
United Federation of Postal Clerks	120,669	162,500	143,000a	
National Association of Letter Carriers, AFL-CIO	153,054	201,000	190,000	232,255
National Association of Special Delivery Messengers	2,207	2,400	2,500b	
National Rural Letter Carriers Association	2,851	43,000	40,000	50,205
National Post Office Mail Handlers, Watchmen, Messengers and Group Leaders, Division of Laborers' International Union of North America, AFL-CIO	16,340	41,180	35,000	47,000
National Federation of Government Employees	29			1,000
National Alliance of Postal and Federal Employees	23,452	32,000	32,000	45,000
National Federation of P. O. Motor Vehicle Employees	5,972	8,500	8,000c	
National Association of P. O. and General Services Maintenance Employees	4,223	21,500	21,500c	
National Postal Union	56,369	65,000	70,000d	
National Association of Postal Supervisors	26,977	32,000	32,000	34,690
National League of Postmasters	8,079	18,000	18,000	12,000
National Association of Postmasters of the U. S.	9,729	29,000	29,000	28,203

a The United Federation of Postal Clerks has become the American Postal Workers Union.

b Employees in the National Association of Special Delivery Messengers are represented by the National Association of Letter Carriers.

c Employees represented by the National Federation of P. O. Motor Vehicle Employees and the National Association of P. O. and General Services Maintenance Employees are represented by other unions, particularly the American Postal Workers Union.

d Many New York postal workers represented by the National Postal Union have joined other unions, particularly the American Postal Workers Union.

Source: Kappel Commission, *Towards Postal Excellence*, Report of the President's Commission on Postal Organization, vol. 4, p. 7.45; vol. 5, p. 19. 1975 estimates were based on interviews with union officials.

regional levels. Except for the National Rural Letter Carriers Association, they are affiliated with the AFL-CIO. The two industrial unions listed in Table 5, the National Postal Union and the National Alliance, do not represent single crafts and, thus, are not accorded national recognition. The National Postal Union consists primarily of clerks in the northeastern and southwestern metropolitan areas. The National Alliance is an industrial union of black workers formed some time ago because of the exclusion of blacks from railway unions. The three management organizations listed at the bottom of Table 5 do not bargain with the service.

Membership in the postal unions is voluntary—that is, employees of a craft are free to join or not to join. They may use the union or some other organization, group, or person to represent them in a grievance. The unions are well established and have remarkably high membership percentages: 98 percent of active-duty carriers and 92 percent of rural carriers belong to their respective unions. As many as 90 percent of all postal employees may be in exclusive bargaining units, compared with 21 percent of other federal employees.

Employees were organized into approximately 20,000 locals in 1964, and it is believed that this number has not changed appreciably since then. Their unions are headed by men with long experience in the postal system. In 1975, as Table 6 shows, postal union leaders averaged twenty-nine years of service in postal operations, a much longer time than most of the top management of the Postal Service.

There are three types of recognition spelled out in Executive Order 10988: *exclusive*, giving the organization chosen by the majority of a unit's employees the right to negotiate on behalf of the unit; *formal*, giving organizations with 10 percent or more of a unit's employment the right to be consulted on personnel policy; and *informal*, giving an organization with less than 10 percent of the employees the right to be heard. The situation would have been unworkable but for the limited scope of collective bargaining given to exclusive representatives. Most of the critical areas of bargaining—wages, hiring, overtime, lay-off strikes, union security, employee benefits—were outside the scope of bargaining before reorganization.[18]

The Post Office interpreted the term bargaining "unit" to mean a particular postal craft, although other readings were possible. The executive order provided for agreements at the national and local levels with consultation at the regional level. As a result, a single employee can be represented by two different unions, one at the national

---

[18] Kappel Commission, *Towards Postal Excellence*, vol. 1, p. 117.

Table 6

NUMBER OF YEARS OF EXPERIENCE OF UNION LEADERS WITH POST OFFICE DEPARTMENT AND POSTAL SERVICE, 1975

Association	Name	Initial Year of Service as Postal Employee
American Postal Workers	Francis S. Filbey	1926
National Association of Letter Carriers	James H. Rademacher	1941
National Rural Letter Carriers Association	Rail M. Rainwater	1947
National Post Office Mail Handlers, Watchmen, Messengers and Group Leaders of Laborers' International Union	Lonnie Johnson	1962
National League of Postmasters	Kenneth Jennings	1961
National Association of Postal Supervisors	Donald W. Ledbetter	1940
National Association of Postmasters	Hal L. Hemmingsen	1961
National Alliance of Postal and Federal Employees	Robert L. White	1943

Source: Postal interviews.

level and one locally. Attempts have been made to bring about unification of postal employee organizations and some consolidation has taken place, as can be seen from Table 5, but the craft classification still dominates. The apparent advantages of unity have been overbalanced by the membership's long acceptance of craft groups.

Before reorganization, postal union leaders thought of their members and the Post Office management as both working for the government. Excluded from union-management negotiations were questions of wages, retirement and fringe benefits, job security, work schedules, job descriptions, assignment of personnel, and technology, as well as organization and budgets. (For a comparison of the issues falling within the scope of bargaining for the Post Office Department and for private industry, see Table 7.) Moreover, the unions were, and still are, denied the usual weapons of work stoppage—strikes, boycotts, and actions to influence suppliers. Congress was where the decisions

Table 7

SCOPE OF BARGAINING BEFORE REORGANIZATION

Subject	Private Industry	Post Office Department
Grievances and adverse actions	YES	YES
Management and union rights	YES	YES
Promotion	YES	YES
Transfers	YES	YES
Seniority	YES	YES
Mediation	YES	YES
Safety and health	YES	YES
Discharge and discipline	YES	YES
Recognition	YES	YES
Higher level pay	YES	Procedures only
Vacations	YES	Scheduling only
Wages	YES	NO
Employee benefits (insurance, etc.)	YES	NO
Guarantee of employment	YES	NO
Hiring	YES	NO
Hours, overtime, and holidays	YES	NO
Layoff-rehiring	YES	NO
Leave of absence	YES	NO
Fact finding	YES	NO
Arbitration	YES	NO
Strikes and lockouts	YES	NO
Training and apprenticeship	YES	NO
Union security	YES	NO
Technology of work	YES	NO

Source: Post Office Department Bureau of Personnel, reproduced in *Towards Postal Excellence*, vol. 4, p. 7.25.

affecting employees were made and where the money was to be found, and that was where unions expended most of their energy. They attempted to influence legislation on behalf of their members by helping their friends in the Congress and punishing their enemies. They also made it clear that postal workers represented votes both directly and through their families and friends. It was alleged that there was at least one postal employee in every precinct in the nation and that postal employees directly affected over 2 million votes. The letter carriers, and particularly those in rural areas, were well situated to affect votes as they went about their daily business of delivering mail house to house. An informal presentation to the potential voter of the postal union's support of or objection to a particular candidate could be important to an election's outcome. The letter carriers' magazine, *The Postal Record*, a union publication distributed to postmen, from time to time printed the names and pictures of congressmen considered friendly on pay raises and other issues. The magazine also railed against congressmen, Post Office employees, and others who opposed their point of view. This identification helped the union to elect its friends and defeat its foes.[19] Political support also took the form of individual donations, volunteer campaign activities by union members and their wives and friends, direct support by postal auxiliaries, and block voting at the time of election. Effective use of this political power as a pressure tool was a cornerstone of union policy.

A member of the House Committee for the Post Office and a known friend of postal employees said in an interview that the 2,500 postal workers in his district represented about 5,000 votes, of which he believed he received 4,000. Another congressman admitted that he felt vulnerable to the mailman. One senator said in an interview, "I can tell you one thing. The postal committees are the best committees there are from which to campaign for reelection."[20]

Political power was crucial to the postal unions, not only to influence Congress on matters of wages and the like but also to have an impact on other matters that indirectly affected the interests of union members. In general, rate bills were supported, for they would produce additional revenue for the Post Office and thus enable Congress to justify a wage increase. But bills to authorize the closing or consolidation of post offices or to increase research and engineering funds for post office mechanization had to be monitored carefully to minimize their impact on postal employment.[21] The major decisions on wages, conditions of employment, and Post Office organization and budget were formulated by the Congress in a process of prolonged tripartite bargaining with the department and the labor organizations, with the latter assuming the major role by virtue of their widespread, numerous, and well-organized constituencies.[22] One measure of union strength with Congress is that few bills opposed by organized labor were enacted.[23]

After the completion of national bargaining with Congress, collective bargaining between the unions and the Post Office took place, within the limits of the National Agreement and the rules, regulations,

---

[19] Ibid., vol. 4, p. 7.65.

[20] Ibid., p. 7.63.

[21] Ibid., p. 7.61.

[22] Ibid., vol. 1, p. 24.

[23] Ibid., p. 121.

and procedures of the Civil Service Commission.[24] The task of administering the national master collective agreements with the several labor unions representing the postal employees belonged to the Bureau of Personnel. In addition, an unofficial system of improvisation and bargaining took place at the local level when the rules were felt to be inadequate. Informal communications between different parts of the postal organization facilitated this improvised bargaining activity. At the regional level no negotiations were permitted. Unions were recognized for consultative and administrative purposes only, although they might advise on personnel procedures and assist in conducting adverse actions. Agreements bargained at the lower level were sometimes inconsistent with each other. Particular matters might be negotiable in one area but not in another. Since the postmaster general placed considerable confidence in the local postmasters, local agreements were not overturned nor were inconsistencies resolved.[25]

There is little evidence in the master agreement that the unions restricted management's right to manage. Few large private enterprises have enjoyed a wider range of management freedom than the Post Office.[26] Congress was reluctant to approve major mechanization and modernization of postal operations because that would affect the number and activity of employees. While in general the unions did not publicly oppose increased mechanization within the department, it is thought that they have influenced Congress on this question.[27]

The Postal Reorganization Act became effective in July 1971. Since then supervisors have been prohibited from performing work falling under the job descriptions of the crafts at post offices with 100 or more bargaining-unit employees. Postal unions at the national level, according to their contract, have to be informed not less than ninety days in advance when major new technology or equipment is to be purchased and installed. A committee composed of equal numbers of management and union representatives is notified of each innovation, and it attempts to resolve any questions about the impact of the proposed change upon affected employees. If these questions are not resolved within a reasonable time, they are given priority in arbitration under the grievance procedures. However, few significant issues affecting cost-efficiency and productivity have reached the discussion stage. It was further agreed by the Postal Service that no employee in the regular work force would be laid off involuntarily because of

---

[24] Ibid., p. 25.
[25] Ibid., vol. 4, p. 7.54.
[26] Ibid., p. 7.59.
[27] Ibid., vol. 1, p. 121; vol. 3, p. 2.24.

mechanization if that employee applied for a new position at his or her former wage level.[28] In commenting on his attempts to improve efficiency, Postmaster General Bailar said that ". . . opposition to our cost-cutting efforts has in most cases far outweighed any support we have received."[29]

All the postal union leaders opposed the reorganization. Although nominally committed to progress, they resisted a new set of rules and a new bargaining situation, probably because the existing situation served their objectives well.[30] They did not wish authority over postal matters to move away from the Congress where they were so powerful. Only upon being offered a substantial increase in postal wages did they change their position. Indeed, union leaders were pushed by their rank and file, who intensely desired the raise.[31] In order to neutralize the most powerful opponent to reorganization and ensure passage of the act, the administration made common cause with the AFL-CIO, by consenting to pay raises totaling more than 14 percent and by providing the AFL-CIO with an opportunity to strengthen itself immensely in the federal sector. The agreement gave the national postal unions increased recognition and moved them one step closer to unionization of all federal employees. In the reorganization, the executive branch gave up its largest source of patronage.[32]

On November 19, 1970, approximately three months after the Postal Reorganization Act was signed into law, labor and management announced their agreement to compress the time required for rank and file employees to reach the top of the pay scale from twenty-one years to eight years,[33] in effect providing a second increase in pay. This move, along with the 14 percent wage increase, greatly increased the attractiveness of postal jobs, as indicated by a decline of more than 50 percent in the already low quit rate between 1969 and 1971 (see Table A-3).

The reorganization agreement was neutral on the right-to-work

---

[28] Agreement between the U.S. Postal Service and American Postal Workers Union, AFL-CIO, National Association of Letter Carriers, AFL-CIO, National Post Office Mail Handlers, Watchmen, Messengers and Group Leaders, Division of Labor, International Union of North America, AFL-CIO, National Rural Letter Carriers Association, July 21, 1973, to July 30, 1975, p. 2, 4, 5.

[29] House, Committee on the Post Office and Civil Service, *Proceedings*, March 15, 1977, p. 12.

[30] Kappel Commission, *Towards Postal Excellence*, vol. 1, p. 14.

[31] Frank Joseph, "Postal Report: Administration Victorious in Long Fight for Basic Reform of Postal Service," *CPR National Journal*, July 4, 1970, p. 1435.

[32] Ibid., pp. 1434 and 1436.

[33] Bruce L. Thorp, "Postal Report: Mail Unions and Government Enter Era of Collective Bargaining," *CPR National Journal*, December 5, 1970, p. 2655.

issue, accepting such laws in the nineteen states that already had them but leaving the matter up to collective bargaining in the other states. It thus raised the possibility of union shops in government. Labor management relations are subject to the National Labor Relations Act, enforceable by the National Labor Relations Board and the federal courts. Unfair labor practice charges in the Postal Service are now handled just as they are in the private sector.[34]

The postal unions are converting from quasi-lobbies to labor activists fully involved in collective bargaining and lacking only the right to strike. They continue to pressure Congress for the right to strike. Since it is unlawful for postal employees to strike, the reorganization provides for binding arbitration in the event of unresolved bargaining impasses to assure parity of bargaining power between labor and management. If no agreement is reached within forty-five days, the Federal Mediation and Conciliation Service must be notified. If the parties fail to reach agreement or to adopt their own procedure for a binding resolution of the dispute by the end of ninety days from the first notice, the Federal Mediation and Conciliation Service must establish a fact-finding panel by submitting to the parties a list of neutral and impartial persons from which each party selects one person. The two so selected choose a third person to serve as chairman of the fact-finding panel. The arbitration board must give the parties a full and fair hearing and report its findings with or without recommendations to the parties to the dispute within forty-five days. Costs of the arbitration board are shared equally by management and labor. Decisions of the arbitration board are conclusive and binding.[35]

Wage Schedules in the Postal Service

The basic pay scales are the Postal Service Schedule (PS) for bargaining-unit employees, the Postal Management Schedule (PMS) for nonbargaining-unit personnel not defined as officers, executives, or professionals, and the Postal Executive Schedule (PES) for Postal Service officers, executives, managers, and professionals. While the PES schedule duplicates the PMS schedule for grade levels 15 through 17, pay increases are granted on a time-progression basis in the PMS and on a merit basis in the PES. The PS schedule (Table 8), which includes all bargaining-unit employees, is the most important one affecting costs and average wages.

---

[34] Joseph, "Postal Report: Administration Victorious," p. 1436.
[35] "Postal Reorganization Act," P.L. 91-375, *Legislative History*, pp. 3652, 3663.

Table 8
POSTAL SERVICE SCHEDULE—FULL-TIME ANNUAL RATES—EFFECTIVE MAY 8, 1976

Level		PS Steps												Step Increments
		1	2	3	4	5	6	7	8	9	10	11	12	
1	New Salary	10,008	10,181	10,354	10,527	10,700	10,873	11,046	11,219	11,392	11,565	11,738	11,911	173
	Base Salary	9,800	9,973	10,146	10,319	10,492	10,665	10,838	11,011	11,184	11,357	11,530	11,703	
2	New Salary	10,427	10,614	10,801	10,988	11,175	11,362	11,549	11,736	11,923	12,110	12,297	12,484	187
	Base Salary	10,219	10,406	10,593	10,780	10,967	11,154	11,341	11,528	11,715	11,902	12,089	12,276	
3	New Salary	10,880	11,082	11,284	11,486	11,688	11,890	12,092	12,294	12,496	12,698	12,900	13,102	202
	Base Salary	10,672	10,874	11,076	11,278	11,480	11,682	11,884	12,086	12,288	12,490	12,692	12,894	
4	New Salary	11,370	11,588	11,806	12,024	12,242	12,460	12,678	12,896	13,114	13,332	13,550	13,768	218
	Base Salary	11,162	11,380	11,598	11,816	12,034	12,252	12,470	12,688	12,906	13,124	13,342	13,560	
5	New Salary	11,902	12,137	12,372	12,607	12,842	13,077	13,312	13,547	13,782	14,017	14,252	14,487	235
	Base Salary	11,694	11,929	12,164	12,399	12,634	12,869	13,104	13,339	13,574	13,809	14,044	14,279	
6	New Salary	12,473	12,728	12,983	13,238	13,493	13,748	14,003	14,258	14,513	14,768	15,023	15,278	255
	Base Salary	12,265	12,520	12,775	13,030	13,285	13,540	13,795	14,050	14,305	14,560	14,815	15,070	
7	New Salary	13,092	13,367	13,642	13,917	14,192	14,467	14,742	15,017	15,292	15,567	15,842	16,117	275
	Base Salary	12,884	13,159	13,434	13,709	13,984	14,259	14,534	14,809	15,084	15,359	15,634	15,909	
8	New Salary	13,761	14,059	14,357	14,655	14,953	15,251	15,549	15,847	16,145	16,443	16,741		298
	Base Salary	13,553	13,851	14,149	14,447	14,745	15,043	15,341	15,639	15,937	16,235	16,533		
9	New Salary	14,485	14,807	15,129	15,451	15,773	16,095	16,417	16,739	17,061	17,383			322
	Base Salary	14,277	14,599	14,921	15,243	15,565	15,887	16,209	16,531	16,853	17,175			
10	New Salary	15,247	15,595	15,943	16,291	16,639	16,987	17,335	17,683	18,031	18,379			348
	Base Salary	15,039	15,387	15,735	16,083	16,431	16,779	17,127	17,475	17,823	18,171			
11	New Salary	16,404	16,790	17,176	17,562	17,948	18,334	18,720	19,106	19,492	19,878			386
	Base Salary	16,196	16,582	16,968	17,354	17,740	18,126	18,512	18,898	19,284	19,670			

Note: New rates include a cost-of-living adjustment of $146 which is included in old rate and $208 added as of May 8, 1976; COLA = $208.
Source: Postal Service assistant postmaster general for employee relations.

In 1966 the Postal Field Schedule (PFS) was used for nonsupervisory employees and, as shown in Table 9, the bulk of the employees were in grade level 4. The PS schedule of rates effective May 8, 1976, is listed in Table 8. The PS schedule is applied to all nonsupervisory employees and is uniform for all installations in the country. The distribution of employees by grade level in 1976 is similar to that in 1966 (see Table 10) except that the major occupations have been moved up one grade. Job reclassification in 1966 moved clerks and carriers from level 4 to 5 and mail expediter and accounting technician from 5 to 6. Some custodians in small post offices remained in level 1, but these are being phased out through attrition. Now the bulk of the custodial employees are in PS levels 2 and 3, mail handlers are in PS level 4, distribution clerks and carriers are in level 5 (with a few in level 6),

Table 9

DISTRIBUTION OF EMPLOYEES ACCORDING TO PFS
SALARY SCHEDULE, 1966

PFS Grade Level	Salary Range[a]	Number of Employees in Each Grade	Percent in Each Grade
20	$22,760–25,800	14	—
19	20,525–25,320	19	—
18	18,530–24,065	19	—
17	16,793–22,076	82	—
16	15,179–19,931	202	—
15	13,736–18,002	404	—
14	12,427–16,315	839	0.1
13	11,274–14,775	1,147	0.1
12	10,202–13,325	5,246	0.7
11	9,221–12,056	5,501	0.8
10	8,345–10,892	10,056	1.5
9	7,665–9,960	14,547	2.2
8	7,088–9,203	13,618	2.0
7	6,545–8,725	21,402	3.2
6	6,113–8,346	12,834	1.9
5	5,697–7,798	35,620	5.4
4	5,331–7,267	431,108	65.6
3	4,919–6,745	64,212	9.7
2	4,552–6,191	26,396	4.0
1	4,204–5,733	5,357	0.8

[a] Prior to the Wage Increase Act of 1967.
Source: Post office manual; Post Office Department, Employment Complement, reproduced in Kappel Commission, *Towards Postal Excellence*, vol. 1, p. 97.

Table 10

POSTAL MANPOWER
(on payroll as of June 30)

Employee Groups	1974	1973	1972	1971	1970	1969
Headquarters employees	2,931	2,531	2,301	2,611	2,883	2,538
Field regular employees:						
Regional and other field units reporting to						
headquarters	10,079	5,128	5,460	5,761	6,663	6,026
Inspection service	5,461	4,680	4,716	2,511	2,112	1,861
Postmasters	30,288	29,490	30,731	29,945	29,679	30,970
Post office supervisors and technical personnel	37,422	34,474	38,102	37,357	37,412	36,741
Post office clerks and mail handlers	243,291	238,727	250,390	239,571	243,090	244,394
City delivery carriers and vehicle drivers	171,460	171,504	174,974	166,006	165,488	163,628
Rural delivery carriers	30,674	30,423	31,024	31,131	31,063	30,945
Special delivery messengers	2,964	2,995	3,205	2,661	2,656	2,869
Building and equipment maintenance personnel	24,708	23,508	23,962	22,768	22,235	21,177
Vehicle maintenance facility personnel	5,289	5,416	5,823	5,589	5,291	5,032
Total regular employees	564,567	548,876	570,688	545,911	548,572	546,181
Total substitute employees	145,866	152,175	135,712	183,000	192,644	192,821
Grand total	710,433	701,051	706,400	728,911	741,216	739,002

Source: *Annual Report of the Postmaster General, 1973-1974*, p. 51.

and equipment and vehicle maintenance personnel are in levels 5 through 12 depending on technical specialties. By far the greatest number of all field personnel are in level 5.

In the PS schedule listed in Table 8 there are from ten to twelve steps associated with each PS level. These steps represent salary increments based on tenure. Step 1 is an entry wage for each level; after one year an employee moves to step 2, assuming satisfactory work performance, and after another year to step 3, and so on until the highest step is reached. These increases are in addition to all bargained increases, which affect the pay figures listed in the table.

A breakdown of the number of employees in each occupational group is given in Table 10. About 80 percent of all postal employees are clustered in a variety of jobs in four occupational groups: mail handlers (PFS-4), clerks (PFS-5), carriers (PFS-5), and motor vehicle operators (PFS-5).

A comparison of the percentage increases in average hourly earnings for postal workers and for manufacturing workers suggests that there has been a tendency for the Post Office/Postal Service to grant its employees greater than average increases. The wages of postal workers increased by 51 percent between fiscal years 1960-1969 (Table 11), compared with an increase of only 33.2 percent for manufacturing employees. For the years 1969-1970 and 1970-1971 the wage increases for postal workers were almost twice as large as those received by manufacturing workers. After slipping back a little in the years 1971-

Table 11

PERCENT CHANGES IN AVERAGE HOURLY WAGES,
1960-1974

	Postal Workers	Manufacturing Workers
1960-1969	51.0%	33.2%
1969-1970	10.7	5.5
1970-1971	11.9	6.4
1971-1972	6.2	6.8
1972-1973	5.8	6.4
1973-1974	12.6[a]	10.0

a For the Postal Service figures, see footnote 36, chapter 2.
Source: The percent changes for manufacturing workers are calculated from average hourly earnings, private nonfarm economy in Tables C-15 and C-17 from issues of *Employment and Earnings*, Bureau of Labor Statistics. Wages increases for postal workers are calculated on a fiscal year basis so the time periods are not strictly comparable.

1973, postal workers then moved ahead with increases of 12.6 percent in 1973-1974 and 15 percent in 1974-1975.[36] From 1970 to 1975, average hourly earnings of postal workers rose by 51 percent while those of private nonfarm workers increased by 40 percent, both exclusive of changes in fringe benefits. (See Figure 2.)

Even before the reorganization and its accompanying sizable wage increases, the salaries of nonsupervisory postal employees were considered to be more than competitive with those paid to similar employees by private companies in most areas.[37] (The postal employee annual quit rate in 1969 was only 13.4 percent while that of manufacturing employees was 32.4 percent.) In 1973, the Postal Service and the unions signed a new National Agreement covering the period from July 21, 1973, to July 20, 1975. As of July 30, 1973, the basic wage increase of postal workers for 1973 was exceeded only by that of workers in the electrical equipment industry, who received a 7.5 percent raise.[38] The postal agreement provided for a $700 a year increase effective July 21, 1973, and another $400 a year effective July 21, 1974. The 90,000 nonunion supervisory workers received a similar increase on November 12, 1973. According to the Cost of Living Council, increases for union members worked out to 6.8 percent in the first year, 3.9 percent in the second. (Also there was an additional 0.9 percent qualified-benefits increase in the first year and 1.2 percent in the second that the council excluded from its computations in determining whether the settlement was consistent with government pay standards—generally holding increases to 3.5 percent a year.) Included in the agreement was an increase in the Postal Service's share of the premium payment for basic life insurance. The agreement also provided for four cost-of-living pay adjustments (COLA) during the two-year period. By November 9, 1974, cost-of-living pay adjustments added another $998.

---

[36] Average hourly wages in 1973, 1974, and 1975 were $5.07, $5.71 and $6.86, respectively. The wage for 1974 was estimated by increasing the 1973 wage by 6.8 percent, the Cost of Living Council's estimate for the basic increase plus the cost-of-living increment of $.30 per hour. The 1975 figure is estimated by adding the basic increment of $400 to the COLA of $1327 for the year. It is then expressed as an hourly increment by dividing it by 2010, the average hours worked annually. This was then added to the 1974 figure.

[37] "Carrier supervisors consistently reported that the average carrier route would be served in six to seven hours instead of the eight hours now assigned to it," George M. Wattles, "The Rates and Costs of the U.S. Postal Service," *Journal of Law and Economics*, vol. 16, no. 1 (April 1973), p. 115; Kappel Commission, *Towards Postal Excellence*, vol. 5, p. 15.

[38] *Annual Report of the Postmaster General, 1972-1973*, p. 19; Margaret Gentry, "Rise Allowed in Mail Rates," *Washington Post*, September 1, 1973; "Labor: The Quiet Front," *Newsweek*, July 30, 1973, p. 57.

Figure 2
AVERAGE SALARIES, 1975 DOLLARS

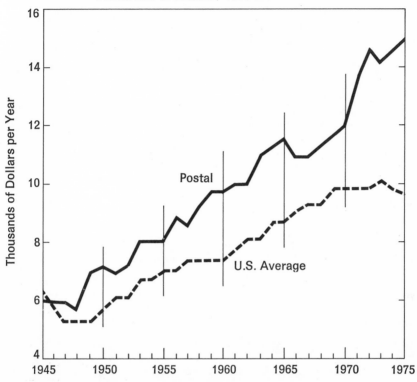

Source: Ewing and Salaman, *The Postal Crisis*, p. 20.

The new labor contract announced on July 21, 1975, gave postal workers $400 per year upon ratification, $250 in March and October 1976, and $600 in July 1977. In addition, postal workers continue to receive the cost-of-living adjustments each May and November of one cent per hour for each 0.4 percent increase in the consumer price index. The increase in health benefits in the new contract will cost the service between $12 million and $15 million per year.[39]

While not indicating conclusively that postal workers are over-paid, the fact that the wage increases for postal workers have been larger than those for manufacturing workers suggests that the former have received favorable wage treatment for the past fifteen years and may now be overpaid. If we examine manufacturing industries whose rates of pay ranked just below (machinery, except electrical) and just

---

[39] *Wall Street Journal*, July 22, 1975, p. 3.

above (ordnance manufacturing and transportation-equipment manufacturing) postal rates of pay in 1958, we find that the wage increases
in these industries from 1958 to 1972, amounting to 80, 63, and 88
percent respectively, fell short of the increase in postal wage rates,
which increased by 100 percent (see Table 12). From statistics compiled by the Postal Service for October-November 1976 in Table 13,
four selected service industries paid an average hourly wage of $5.39
while the Postal Service paid $7.20, which is 33.6 percent higher. If
postal workers were not underpaid in 1958, and the data presented in
chapter 6 indicate they were not, then the figures suggest they may
have become overpaid by 1976. This assumes that there were in this
period no special circumstances like a need to expand postal employ-

Table 12

WAGE LEVELS AND PERCENTAGE INCREASES BY INDUSTRY GROUP

Industry	Mean (1)	1972 (2)	1958 (3)	Percentage Increase, 1958-1972 (4)
Petroleum and coal products	$3.51	$4.95	$2.73	81
Primary metal products	3.35	4.66	2.64	77
Transportation equipment	3.37	4.73	2.51	88
Ordnance and accessories	3.13	4.09	2.51	63
Postal Service	3.21	4.79	2.39	100
Machinery, except electrical	3.11	4.27	2.37	80
Chemicals and allied products	3.03	4.20	2.29	83
Lumber and wood products	2.92	3.99	2.25	77
Rubber and plastics	2.72	3.60	2.19	64
Instruments and related products	2.77	3.72	2.15	73
Stone, clay, and glass products	2.78	3.91	2.12	84
Electrical machinery	2.72	3.67	2.12	73
Paper and paper products	2.80	3.94	2.10	88
Food and kindred products	2.58	3.60	1.94	86
Miscellaneous manufacturing industries	2.29	3.11	1.79	74
Furniture and fixtures	2.26	3.06	1.78	72
Tobacco and tobacco products	2.24	3.43	1.59	116
Leather and leather products	2.00	2.71	1.56	74
Apparel and other textile products	1.95	2.61	1.54	69
Textile mill products	1.98	2.73	1.49	83

Source: Author's calculations.

Table 13

COMPARISON OF GROSS EARNINGS PER PAID HOUR FOR
NONSUPERVISORY POSTAL SERVICE EMPLOYEES WITH
THOSE OF SELECTED PRIVATE SERVICE INDUSTRIES,
OCTOBER-NOVEMBER 1976

Industry	Gross Earnings per Paid Hour
Banking	$3.72
Insurance	4.58
Telephone communications	6.56
Electric utilities	6.69
Average	5.39
Postal Service	7.20

Source: Data for the selected private industries are from the Bureau of Labor Statistics, Employment and Earnings Series, October 1976. This table is compiled from the U.S. Postal Service's *Comprehensive Statement on Postal Operations*, presented to the Committees on Post Office and Civil Service and the Committees on Appropriations of the Senate and House of Representatives pursuant to 39 U.S.C. 2401(g), as added by P.L. No. 94-421, p. 6.

ment much more rapidly than employment in the industries with comparable pay.

Before the reorganization act, Congress controlled postal wages and benefits. Both the postal unions and Post Office Department lobbied Congress for changes they thought should be made. The big mailers also took part in the process. Although unions and the Postal Service now deal directly with each other, temptations still exist for the unions to go back to Congress for help if necessary. A top union official has said that Congress is still very much in the picture and that if management were to try to reduce mail delivery to five days a week, unions might try to keep it at six. More recently the unions have been lobbying Congress for the right to strike. Moreover, big mailers, who once had no influence on the bargaining that affected their rate subsidies and who regarded themselves as victims waiting on the sidelines to pay the bill for the results,[40] now (with the Administrative Procedure and Postal Reorganization acts), can present economic and accounting data before the Postal Rate Commission in rate increase cases.

The bargaining relationship between the Postal Service and its employees was the first for federal labor and management and was

---

[40] Thorp, "Postal Report: Mail Unions," pp. 2658, 2659.

intended to become an example for labor-management relationship elsewhere in the federal government. Agreements on wages, working conditions, and benefits were expected to set patterns for settlements elsewhere.

Those sympathetic with this development are concerned whether collective bargaining with binding arbitration can settle disputes at various levels of government where employees are forbidden to strike. The postal experience, still very limited, will show whether this system can be successful in government.[41]

One danger of compulsory arbitration is that it delegates to a third party decisions affecting costs which must be paid out of public funds. Such a procedure encourages both parties to make inflated demands in the expectation of an arbitrated compromise. It thus tends to have a stultifying effect on collective bargaining as both parties hope to convince the arbitrator more readily than they can convince each other. Edward B. Miller, chairman of the National Labor Relations Board, said that excessive dependence on arbitration would mark the end of free collective bargaining in the public sector and signify that the experiment had failed. If either side comes to regard the discussions across the table as a mere prelude to litigation before an arbitrator or an arbitration board, collective bargaining in the government sector will have become a mockery.[42]

---

[41] Ibid., pp. 2659 and 2657.
[42] Ibid., p. 2658.

3

WAGE RATES AND QUIT RATES

If in the same neighborhood, there was an employment evidently either more or less advantageous than the rest, so many people would crowd into it in the one case, and so many would desert it in the other that its advantages would soon return to the level of other employment. . . . Pecuniary wages . . . are . . . extremely different. . . . But this difference arises partly from certain circumstances in the employments themselves . . . which make up for a small pecuniary gain in some and counter-balance a great one in others . . . and partly from the policy which no-where leaves things at perfect liberty.

Adam Smith, *The Wealth of Nations.*

Postal Wages

Since reorganization, postal wage rates have been set through negotiations between the Postal Service and the unions representing the various postal crafts. The basic average hourly wage rates for annual-rate regular employees are listed in Table 14. The 1976 pay structure has entry rates ranging from $10,008 in level 1 to $16,404 in level 11, a compressed range compared with that used before reorganization. The ratio of top to bottom entry rates decreased from 2.27 in 1972 to 1.64 in late 1976. In the levels up to PS-8, which contain 95 percent of the field service employees, the intervals between levels are about 5 percent. In levels from PS-8 to PS-11 the intervals are about 6 percent. Within each of the lower levels there is a series of twelve steps; within each of the higher levels, ten steps. These steps are at intervals of 1.5 to 2 percent in the lower grades, 2.1 to 2.4 percent in the higher

Table 14

BASIC AVERAGE HOURLY WAGE RATES FOR ANNUAL RATE REGULAR EMPLOYEES BY CRAFT

Craft	1972[a]	1974[b]
Custodial and protective employees	$3.91	$5.26
Distribution clerks and mail handlers	4.73	6.08
City carriers	4.81	6.20
Rural route carriers	4.81	6.20
Special delivery messengers	4.82	6.22
Vehicle service drivers	4.86	6.28
Maintenance–motor vehicle service	5.00	6.43
Maintenance–postal equipment	5.01	6.44

[a] J. G. Tiedemann, Personnel Research Division, U.S. Postal Service (unpublished manuscript).
[b] See Tables 8 and 11, November 9, 1974.

grades. The maximum pay in a given grade is 22 to 24 percent above the minimum. The step increases are awarded at regular intervals, are unrelated to productivity, and are over and above the general pay raises employees receive as a result of bargaining.

Before reorganization, step increases were given annually for six years in the lower grades and every three years thereafter until the top was reached in twenty-one years. In level 8 the top was reached in eighteen years; in levels 9-19, in fifteen years; in level 20, in nine years, and in level 21, in four years. On November 19, 1970, as a result of negotiation after passage of the Postal Reorganization Act but before it took effect, the time required to reach the top was shortened.

Except for professional, scientific, or managerial personnel who accept employment with the Postal Service in regional, district, or headquarters positions, new employees are always appointed to step 1 of the salary level. There is little wage distinction or promotion within a craft to differentiate more difficult assignments or higher degrees of skill. Neither is there any practical financial incentive to improve efficiency on the job as long as one remains a clerk or carrier. Only seniority yields better working conditions, preferable tours of duty, and step increases. This arrangement discourages capable employees from volunteering for more responsible positions. In fact, they often "bid off" successive assignments until they reach the easiest assignment for which they are eligible. For example, senior postal clerks often bid off assignments requiring complex scheme knowledge, leaving these to less experienced employees.

Because of the step increases in the wage schedule, it takes only three years of in-grade increases for a postal worker entering at level PS-5 to exceed the entry level of the next higher grade. He usually has to reach the eighth step in his level to be considered for promotion. By the time he has served eleven years his pay is above the entry wage of a job four levels higher. Since he is guaranteed only a two-step increase upon promotion (around $400 to $500 per year depending upon grade level), he may not regard this as sufficient extra compensation for the additional responsibility. Promotion to a supervisory position is guaranteed a three-step increase along with the grade level increase. But it is not unusual for a new supervisor to be assigned to a different installation, or to a night shift, or to be rotated among work crews. Consequently, employees sometimes decline a promotion to first-line supervisory if the new responsibilities are unknown and demanding compared with those of a clerk or carrier. This system frustrates management and fails to satisfy even ardent supporters of the Postal Service.

A night differential rate 10 percent higher than the basic hourly rate is paid for work performed between 6:00 p.m. and 6:00 a.m. Annual-rate regulars, hourly rate regulars, and part-time, flexible-schedule employees at PS-11 and below receive overtime compensation at 150 percent of the base pay rate for work performed in excess of forty hours a week or in excess of eight hours a day. Employees at PMS-19 to 23 (postmasters, inspectors, and rural carriers excepted) receive compensatory time off equal to the overtime worked. There is a Sunday differential of 25 percent that all employees except casuals receive. Work performed by full-time regular employees on holidays is compensated at double time.

The average contribution for fringe benefits in the Postal Service is 32.1 percent of its payroll for 1976-1977 while the corresponding figure for all industries is 30.0 percent. The principal fringe benefits are for time off, retirement, health, welfare and social security, and special benefits such as employee awards and uniform allowances. In Table 15 these are expressed as percentages of base salary and compared with private industry, whose figures are calculated for 1975. The time-off benefits as a percentage of payroll for the Postal Service are almost twice as high as for all industries, while postal benefits in other categories are slightly less.

Past studies have indicated that the pool of individuals interested in and available for employment in the Postal Service is large enough

Table 15

COMPARISON OF FRINGE BENEFITS
(percent of payroll)

	Postal Service 1976-1977	All Industries 1975
Time-off benefits	18.3	9.4
Retirement programs	7.1	9.0
Health and welfare programs	6.2	10.5
Special benefits (for example, uniform allowances, service and suggestion awards, bonuses, et cetera)	.5	1.1
Total	32.1	30.0

Source: Percents for the Postal Service are calculated from year-to-date figures in the U.S. Postal Service, *National Payroll Hours Summary Report* for the accounting periods ending February 25, 1977. Figures for all industries were taken from the Chamber of Commerce, *Employee Benefits 1975* (Washington, D.C., 1976), p. 30.

to meet any foreseeable manpower needs.[1] Its wages are amply competitive with other users of semiskilled and unskilled manpower, even in most large northern and western labor markets, to attract a sufficient number of new workers. Thus it is not likely to face manpower shortages except perhaps in the largest cities where wage levels are more competitive.

The wages of blue-collar workers employed by the federal government are determined administratively by their agencies and are adjusted to prevailing wages in the area. In contrast, postal workers draw increasingly higher pay at regular intervals in addition to general increases negotiated with postal unions and promotions, and the scales are uniform nationally. There is no decisive evidence from comparisons with pay rates in other jobs, private or federal, that postal workers are underpaid or overpaid. To determine this, we must turn to the evidence of voluntary quit rates.

Factors Affecting the Quit Rate

Labor mobility can be characterized in terms of (1) the causal basis of separations: voluntary quits or involuntary separations; (2) the desti-

---

[1] Kappel Commission, *Towards Postal Excellence*, vol. 4, p. 5.16.

nation of labor flow, including withdrawals from the labor force, new occupations, or new employers in the labor market; and (3) the cause of the flow. The statistic that best measures voluntary labor mobility is the quit rate.[2] This is the number of "quits" per month or year for each 100 employees. Quits are voluntary terminations of employment by employees for any reason except retirement, transfer to another establishment of the same firm, or service in the armed forces. Statistics on the quit rate are available on a continuing and current basis and are the most useful labor mobility data available for our purpose.

Most job changes are complex in nature, involving changes of employer, industry, occupation, or geographical area, or some combination of these. In a study of six cities between 1940 and 1949, it was found that approximately 50 percent of all job shifts involved the simultaneous change of employer, occupation, and industry. About 20 percent involved simultaneous changes of employer and industry, and about 20 percent involved a simple movement among firms without a change in occupation or industry. Five percent were changes in both employer and occupation.[3] Many aspects of labor mobility like job changes or relocations within the same firm are not measured by the quit rate. Absenteeism is not captured in the quit rate although it may well be a symptom of the same dissatisfactions that lead an employee to quit.

Adam Smith's view of the factors affecting quit rates is quoted at the beginning of this chapter.[4] Smith merely said that there was a tendency for workers to choose jobs according to their relative attractiveness. He did not try to quantify or explain this tendency. In the current literature examining the factors influencing the quit rate, observers are divided into two camps. Some, like Professor Simon Rot-

---

[2] It has been suggested to me by Professor H. Gregg Lewis that the quit rate is an ambiguous statistic since it contains not only those workers which have quit "voluntarily" but also those who have been "encouraged" to quit by their employers and yet are still counted as "voluntary." Among professionals the distinction between "voluntary" and "involuntary" is often blurred because "voluntary" resignations may well be forced. This ambiguity is of little importance for the Postal Service because supervisors have such difficulty firing postal workers. Neither would I expect this difficulty to be serious for *nonsupervisory* workers in most other industries. If the ambiguous portion of total quits is small and stable, the quit-rate statistic can be profitably used. The fact that the quit rate behaves predictably over the business cycle suggests that it is at least as good as many other frequently used economic statistics.

[3] Herbert S. Parnes, "The Labor Force and Labor Markets," *Employment Relations Research*, Herbert G. Heneman, Jr. et al., eds. (New York: Harper and Brothers, 1960), pp. 16-33.

[4] Adam Smith, *The Wealth of Nations* (New York: The Modern Library, 1937), Book 1, chapter 10.

tenberg, emphasize the influence of wage levels and competitive forces. Others, like Neil Chamberlain, emphasize the lack of information and other apparent market imperfections.[5] The question remains, to what extent do workers make comparisons among alternatives and move to those positions where their net advantage is maximized?

Studies of workers' attitudes and job choices suggest that workers have multiple and complex goals and that their choices are bounded by their knowledge of the alternatives. Professor Stigler has said that because the number of potential employers for an unskilled or semi-skilled worker is in the millions, no worker can become informed on the prospective earnings that could be obtained from every one of these potential employers.[6] A worker will search for wage offers until the expected marginal return equals the marginal cost of search. A worker places more trust in information from a friend who does the same kind of work than in information from most commercial sources, so he is apt to concentrate his efforts on a very few opportunities suggested to him by friends.[7]

Unfortunately for the firm with a turnover problem, a worker leaving is often unwilling or unable to tell the management why. The real reason may be totally different from the one he articulates. Perhaps he does not really know why himself. More often there is no single reason but rather a whole cluster of reasons. He may not want to discuss it at all. He may be reluctant to say he's leaving because the boss has not said hello to him for a week. He may not want to tell the real reason because it might be considered tattling. He might even refrain from telling the truth for fear it would stand in the way of his getting a good reference.[8] For these reasons the results of exit interviews are often nondescript and of scant value.

Even if the interviewee is open and honest, his reply may not be useful to the firm in changing its policy. For instance, it is difficult to think how a firm could make use of the following reasons given by employees upon resignation:

> "I wanted an extra day off to go to a picnic. The boss wouldn't give it to me so I quit."

---

[5] See Simon Rottenberg, "On Choice in Labor Markets," *Industrial and Labor Relations Reviews*, vol. 9, no. 2 (January 1956), pp. 183-99; Neil W. Chamberlain, *The Labor Sector* (New York: McGraw-Hill, 1965), pp. 366-74.

[6] George J. Stigler, "Information in the Labor Market," *Journal of Political Economy*, vol. 70, supplement (October 1962), pp. 94-95.

[7] Albert Rees, "Information Networks in Labor Markets," *American Economic Review*, vol. 56, supplement (May 1966), pp. 560, 562.

[8] Frederick G. Gaudet, *Labor Turnover: Calculation and Costs*, AMA Research Study 39 (New York: American Management Association, 1960), p. 86.

"I did not want to be transferred to another department; there was nobody to talk to except some women and girls."

"The foreman said my pony-tail hairdo was awful and to change it. I said 'no' and that was that. Anyway he was married."

"The boss fired a friend of mine. I told him I'm fired too."

"I asked my boss to lend me a dollar. He said all he could spare was fifty cents, so I quit."

"I was driving a truck for a perfume factory but they put me inside filling bottles. I went home every night smelling of gardenias and violets. My wife understood. But one night I got in a subway near six other guys. They all sniffed and looked at me and returned glances at each other with funny smiles. That was enough for me."[9]

These workers are not so much stating reasons as describing the incidents that provoked them to quit jobs they must already have regarded as only marginally satisfying. It is hard to believe that any of these people would have quit—except perhaps the perfume bottler —if they had thought they were reasonably well paid. One study based on exit interviews found that 40 percent of employees who quit said that pay was the most important reason for quitting. Promotion, also in part a pay factor, was the next most important reason; it was cited in 34 percent of the interviews.[10]

Raising the wage rate is not the only way quits can be reduced. Changes in personnel policies have reduced quits.[11] Exit interviews have inspired many recommendations for reducing labor turnover such as teaching foreign-born workers to speak English, improving housing facilities, and legal aid.

The attitudes, recruiting policies, and hiring practices of employers are important factors affecting the quit rate, as are the physical characteristics of the job, the employee's evaluation of his relation with his supervisor and fellow workers, the steadiness of work, and the degree of interest the work generates among employees.[12] Personal circumstances—age, sex, race, marital status, degree of skill, geographical location, and home ownership—influence the decision to quit. For instance, women have been more prone to quit jobs than men.

---

[9] Ibid., p. 88, quoting "Why They Quit," compiled by Jeffrey Ford, *New York Times Magazine*, May 17, 1953.

[10] Gaudet, *Labor Turnover*, p. 87, quoting Frank J. Smith and Willard A. Kerr, "Turnover Factors as Assessed by the Exit Interview," *Journal of Applied Psychology*, vol. 37 (October 1953), pp. 352-55.

[11] Gaudet, *Labor Turnover*, p. 84.

[12] Parnes, "The Labor Force and Labor Markets," p. 27.

This may be so because they are employed predominantly in the lower wage industries,[13] and because theirs is often the second, less critical source of income for the family. The quit rate is also influenced by collective bargaining agreements, union policies, informal agreements among employers, and government action.[14]

The quit rate for nonwhites has been greater than for whites.[15] Skilled workers have been less apt to quit than unskilled workers, and workers of higher social standing less apt to quit than those of lower status.[16] Because fewer positions are available to them, employees in the South and in rural areas have been less apt to quit than employees in the North and in urban areas. There is a decline in quits as age increases, which reflects both a period of job shopping by young workers and older workers' fear of discriminatory hiring. The inverse relationship between length of service and the quit rate has been well documented.[17]

Some factors that influence labor mobility are under the control of public policy. For example, the extent of unionism and the information-disseminating activities of employment services are factors related to the quit rate, the former inversely and the latter directly. Seniority arrangements under unionism have reduced quit rates.[18] Some observers argue that seniority schemes and pension plans inhibit mobility by enhancing job security and raising wages above the market level. It is also argued that unions reduce mobility by removing many of the grievances at the place of work.[19] In empirical studies the variable indicating the degree of unionization is significant in explaining the quit rate, and with the expected sign, until the wage level variable is added to the regression. The reason for this is that when union power is instrumental in pushing up wages, it becomes difficult to differentiate the union impact from the wage impact.[20]

---

[13] Paul A. Armknecht and John F. Early, "Quits in Manufacturing—A Study of Their Causes," *Monthly Labor Review*, November 1972; Bureau of Labor Statistics, Reprint 2844, p. 33; Parnes, "The Labor Force and Labor Markets," p. 35.

[14] Parnes, "The Labor Force and Labor Markets," p. 14.

[15] Simon Rottenberg, "On Choice in Labor Markets," *Industrial and Labor Relations Review*, vol. 9 (January 1956), p. 207. See Lowell E. Gallaway, "Inter-Industry Labor Mobility among Men 1957-60," in *S.S. Bulletin*, vol. 29 (September 1966), p. 22.

[16] John E. Parker and John F. Burton, Jr., "Voluntary Labor Mobility in the U.S. Manufacturing Sector," *Proceedings of the Industrial Relations Research Association*, Winter 1967, p. 63; John E. Parker and John F. Burton, Jr., "There Is a New Industrial Feudalism" (unpublished manuscript), p. 113.

[17] Parnes, "The Labor Force and Labor Markets," p. 21.

[18] Ibid., pp. 24 and 25.

[19] Parker and Burton, "There Is a New Industrial Feudalism," p. I-2.

[20] Ibid., p. III-1.

Seasonal industries offer lower job security and attract more casual workers; as a result these show a higher proportion of quits.[21] Production workers are more prone to quit when their work is hazardous, when they lack opportunity for promotion, or when they received poor supervision or low wages.

While the theoretical impact of industrial concentration is not universally acknowledged, an inverse relationship between concentration and quits seems probable on the basis of several factors. Increasing concentration in an industry is usually associated with larger firms that pay higher wage rates and provide more training opportunities than smaller firms. More concentrated industries also appear to be able to attract higher quality workers who tend to be less prone to quit.[22] Larger firms offer better chances for internal advancement of employees and tend to be more heavily unionized, with higher wages, extensive seniority provisions, and fringe benefit programs.[23] All these tend to reduce quits.

Whether workers quit for the opportunity of higher earnings alone, or for want of advancement, security, or more interesting work, is still a mystery. The decision to quit results from a complex combination, probably unique with every individual, of the motivational factors already discussed, within the context of the opportunities offered to the worker to shift jobs.[24] Because of the numerous variables that affect the quit rate, it is unlikely that the relative importance of all factors can be separated and evaluated by statistical techniques.

Yale Brozen argues that the quit rate for a given firm may be its best indicator of whether wages are too low or too high.[25] He reasons that workers seldom quit jobs in appreciable numbers unless more attractive jobs are available. It follows that a relatively high quit rate may be generated by the availability of better paying or more attractive jobs elsewhere. In order to retain a work force, then, a firm may have to increase its wage rate or enhance the value of its jobs by other means. Increased wage rates can and do serve as a substitute for other

---

[21] Parker and Burton, "Voluntary Labor Mobility in the U.S. Manufacturing Sector," p. 3.

[22] Parker and Burton, "There Is a New Feudalism," p. II-2.

[23] Ibid., p. III-4.

[24] Charles A. Meyer, "Patterns of Labor Mobility," *Manpower in the U.S., Problems and Policies* (New York: Harper and Brothers, 1954), p. 165.

[25] Yale Brozen, "Wage Rates, Minimum Wage Laws, and Unemployment," *New Individualist Review*, vol. 4, no. 3 (Spring 1966), pp. 30-32. See also H. C. Simons, "Some Reflections on Syndicalism," in *Economic Policy for a Free Society* (Chicago: University of Chicago Press, 1948), pp. 140-41.

desirable terms of employment, or compensate for the unattractive features of a job.

On the other hand, a business should pay only as much as it must to obtain and retain the labor force of the skill and quality it requires. To pay more is to become to the same degree a philanthropic operation. Any company paying higher wages than necessary misallocates resources and is not serving its customers and stockholders well. How long a business can survive doing so depends on the tolerance of its stockholders or the advantages it enjoys in the market. The indicator of whether its wage level is in fact too high is the quit rate.

In a study using forty-nine industries in an interindustry model, John F. Burton, Jr., and John E. Parker found a negative relationship between the wage level and the quit rate such that a one dollar increase in the hourly wage level was associated with a decline of 1.12 percentage points in the monthly quit rate.[26] Melvin Lurie, in his study of transit workers with the Boston Metropolitan Transit Authority, found that the average annual quit rate before unionization in 1904-1911 was 24.1 percent; after unionization and an increase in the relative wage rate in 1913-1916 it fell to 7.8 percent; after public subsidies were provided in 1920-1929 it dropped to only 1.9 percent. This suggests not only that the union was effective in raising the wages of its members but also that public subsidization made it easy for workers to obtain excessive wages.[27]

With minor changes the same scenario can be applied to the Postal Service unions. From 1958-1974 (excluding 1964 and 1965, for which figures are unavailable) the annual average postal quit rate was 7.74. The Carmen's Union was effective in raising the wages of its members 20 percent above what they would have been in the union's absence. The Post Office/Postal Service has been similarly successful. Neither the transit operators nor postal workers were highly skilled; neither were they kept from quitting by an overly generous pension plan.

In the case of the Carmen's Union, as with the postal unions, the most important condition enabling the union to raise wages to excessive levels was the inelasticity of demand indicated by the unavailability of close substitutes. This was achieved in the public transportation business in Boston by barring potential competitors from the market.

[26] John F. Burton, Jr., and John E. Parker, "Interindustry Variations in Voluntary Labor Mobility," *Industrial and Labor Relations Review*, vol. 22, no. 2 (January 1969), p. 213.

[27] Melvin Lurie, "Government Regulations and Union Power: A Case Study of the Boston Transit Industry," *Journal of Law and Economics*, vol. 3 (October 1960), p. 127, pp. 122-34.

Similarly for the Postal Service the Private Express Statutes, which preserve the monopoly of the Postal Service in the delivery of first-class mail, are important for eliminating competitors and maintaining excessive wage levels. Given the barrier to entry, the MTA and the Postal Service have been able to pass on the higher costs of excessive wages in the form of higher fares or rates charged customers. The more inelastic the demand for the service, the more successful a union can be in pushing wages above competitive levels without suffering the consequences of large decreases in the employment of its members. If the demand for transit or postal services is inelastic, an aggressive union can push wages upward with the expectation that fares or rates will be allowed to rise sufficiently to cover the increased costs.

Regulation allows wage increases to be passed on to third parties. The tendency to pass costs on to groups not represented in the bargaining exists not only in the Postal Service but also in regulated freight transportation, public utilities, air transportation of passengers, and other industries which are regulated or protected by the government. The MTA and the Postal Service are required to petition for permission to raise fares or rates. Cost increases due to increased wages are strong prima facie evidence for approval of fare increases; and a fare increase in response to a cost increase can become almost automatic. Despite the shrinking demand for transit service, the Carmen's Union was effective for over forty years. In the early period the union was able to push wage rates above market-required levels since the monopoly transit system could recover its increased costs through fare increases. It became increasingly difficult to do this, as the automobile became a stronger competitor for intracity transportation and the price elasticity of demand for transit service increased. The power of the Carmen's Union diminished as the elasticity of demand for transit service increased. For postal services, the erosion of monopoly in the delivery of first-class mail does not appear to be as great because of the absence of close substitutes; however, electronic transfers may alter the situation radically.

When the MTA started losing its ability to finance excessive wage levels through fare increases, it achieved access to public funds. At this point the costs of excessive wages could be passed on to taxpayers instead of being financed solely by fare increases. At the discretion of private and then, in 1931, political authority, tax assessment was substituted for higher fares as a revenue-providing technique. Increased effectiveness of the Carmen's Union was related to the passage of the Public Control Act, which enabled the Carmen's Union to escape the discipline of the market by financing the deficit from gen-

61

eral tax revenues. While the union did not favor the Public Control Act when it was passed in 1918, by 1930 it had perceived its value and supported a resolution favoring its extension. With regard to the Postal Service, reliance on government revenue generated from taxes to cover deficits has had a long history. This source of revenue, however, was supposed to diminish after reorganization.

In the event that the MTA disregarded the fact that increases in wage costs could be financed from taxes and bargained to hold the line on wages, the union had the option of calling for arbitration with the expectation of more favorable treatment by an arbitration board. This threat of compulsory arbitration and the assessment of operating deficits upon taxpayers was used by the union as a wedge for obtaining wage increases that the company might not have voluntarily granted. When the union asked for compulsory arbitration it expected the arbitration board to be more impressed than the company bargainers by the fact that wage increases would ultimately be paid by taxpayers.

The composition and method for selecting the arbitration board to consider the Carmen's Union's demands were important factors influencing the power of the union to raise wages. The method of selecting the arbitration board made it likely that the decision of the board would be favorable to the union. The agreement provided for one arbitrator to be chosen by the MTA and the Carmen's Union respectively. These two arbitrators selected a third. Since the third arbitrator was crucial to the process, this procedure extended the original conflict to the selection of the third arbitrator. After a number of arbitrations it became increasingly difficult to agree on a third arbitrator who was familiar with the Boston operation. Company officials said that the pressure for getting the arbitration underway forced them to accept an arbitrator from a list constructed by the union. In order to prevent stalemates in the selection of an arbitrator, the Massachusetts legislature empowered the Superior Court to appoint an arbitrator. The Boston Carmen's Union became the beneficiary of this selection process. The arbitration process designed to set wages facilitated the establishment of excessive wages because the union was able to control a majority on the "arbitration" panel.

In the Postal Service an arbitration process has been set up to mediate in disputes that cannot be resolved by bargaining between the postal unions and the Postal Service management. It is foolish to think that the postal unions will fail to use this process to their own advantage when they perceive its benefits. While it is too early to predict a pattern, the regular use of the arbitration procedure would signal the end of meaningful collective bargaining for government employees and the beginning of the use of a new source of power to raise wages. Consequently there is little hope that, as a result of reorganization, excessive wages will be eliminated, and they have not been to date.

Voluntary Quits in the Postal Service

Job vacancies can arise because of quits, firings, deaths, retirements, or promotions. Table 16 breaks down separations in the Postal Service for fiscal years 1974-1975 and 1975-1976 into these categories. Technically, "separations" are personnel actions that result in employees being removed from the rolls of the Postal Service or being transferred to another establishment of the Postal Service. "Termination" describes the separation of a temporary employee because his services are no longer required or for any other reason not specifically covered by another type of personnel action.

During fiscal years 1974-1975 and 1975-1976, the Postal Service had an average gross turnover of 16.2 and 17.2 percent, respectively, of its labor force. Of these separations, deaths and retirements accounted for 15.7 and 17.5 percent, respectively, in years 1974-1975 and 1975-1976. Only 7 and 6 percent of the separations in years 1974-1975 and 1975-1976 were for cause. Voluntary quits made up

Table 16
SEPARATIONS FROM THE POSTAL SERVICE

	FY 1975	FY 1976
Total "nonsupervisory" employees[a]	653,240	639,855
Total separations	105,956 (16.2%)	110,244 (17.2%)
Deaths	2,183 (.3%)	2,176 (.3%)
Retirement	14,541 (2.2)	17,213 (2.7)
Quits	34,049 (5.2)	27,382 (4.3)
Removal for cause	7,935 (1.2)	6,807 (1.1)
Other	47,248 (7.2)	56,666 (8.9)

[a] At beginning of year. Includes "supervisory" employees in the regional offices and other select groups which could not be eliminated because of the design of the data retrieval system. Includes all casual employees. Does not include headquarters employees.
Source: J. G. Tiedemann, Employee and Labor Relations Group, U.S. Postal Service.

Table 17
ANNUAL SEPARATION RATES

	Postal	Federal	All Manufacturing
1970	20.34%	21.84%	57.96%
1971	15.12	18.72	50.16
1972	15.00	20.00	50.10

Source: J. G. Tiedemann, Personnel Research Division, U.S. Postal Service.

32 percent of the separations in 1974-1975 and 25 percent in 1975-1976.

The annual separation rates for postal, federal, and all manufacturing employees are listed in Table 17. The separation rate in the federal service is only about 40 percent as large as the rate in private manufacturing; in the Postal Service it is about 33 percent. Among the thirty-three federal agencies reporting separation data, only three, the Department of the Interior, the Department of Agriculture, and the Tennessee Valley Authority, experienced higher separation rates than the average for all manufacturing industries.

The disparities between the private and public sectors are even more pronounced when quits or voluntary separations are examined. The quit rate for federal service is about 70 percent below that for all manufacturing; the quit rate for the Postal Service is 75 percent below that for all manufacturing. Comparative quit rates for 1972 are listed in Table 18.

In the Postal Service, temporary and part-time employees have a higher turnover than other groups and, in the opinion of some, are considered to be lower quality employees. Temporary employees, which are included in the labor force statistics, serve an apprenticeship of from three to six months and then are routinely replaced. This practice tends to raise the overall turnover rate. The combined turn-

Table 18
ANNUAL QUIT RATES, 1972

Postal Service	6.7%
Federal	8.4
All manufacturing	26.8

Source: J. G. Tiedemann, Personnel Research Division, U.S. Postal Service.

over rate for "temp and subs" in 1966 was around 68 percent—34.5 percent for "subs," 85.4 percent for "temps." The turnover rate for career employees was 7.6 percent per year. Substitutes thus had a turnover rate four times that of regulars, and the rate for temporaries was eleven times as high.[28] Substitutes make up 21 percent of the clerk–carrier–mail handler work force, yet account for 52 percent of its separations.

Reasons for Postal Quits

The postal manual suggests that all employees voluntarily separating should be interviewed to try to retain satisfactory employees and to uncover poor job conditions that need corrective measures. Since most employees either do not work the day tour or work at remote locations, exit interviews are inconvenient and are seldom pursued. For those interviews conducted the data indicate that in 55 percent of the quits the reasons given concerned matters within management's control; 45 percent did not. Of the former, insufficient pay was mentioned 23 percent of the time; lack of advancement, 32 percent; working schedules and requirements, 25 percent; limited training opportunities, 5 percent; and human relations problems, 14 percent.

In the Post Office working conditions were somewhat inferior to those of many other industries. Twelve percent of departing employees said that poor physical working conditions either caused or contributed to their decision to quit. Many post offices were built in the 1930s or before, when mail volume was less than half of what it is today. Employees quitting these installations frequently complained in their exit interviews about crowded and noisy work areas, inadequate locker space and rest rooms, poor lighting, poor heating and cooling systems, excessive noise and heat from mail-processing equipment, and insufficient janitorial service. In Chicago's south suburban facility, perhaps the most outmoded post office in the country, the turnover rate was much higher than in Detroit's modern post offices, with enclosed docks, excellent lighting, adequate parking, and many other features that enhance the working environment.

At some facilities the parking lots are too small so employees are forced to walk long distances through unsafe areas and risk being assaulted. The problem is even more acute when women employed as clerks or mail handlers are assigned night-shift duty at facilities located tion, the Postal Service has been correcting such conditions through its

---

[28] Kappel Commission, *Towards Postal Excellence*, vol. 4, p. 5.89.

in or near poorly lighted areas—they usually quit. Since reorganiza-
Working Conditions Improvement Program. In fiscal 1973, for instance, $27 million was committed to improve plant heating, ventila-
tion, lighting, and other conditions affecting the work atmosphere.
The Working Conditions Improvement Program, concluded during
fiscal 1976, resulted in 99 percent of postal employees working in what
were or would soon be, satisfactory facilities.

The policy of no sex discrimination is responsible for some of
the turnover. In Chicago quite a few of the men assigned to the truck
terminal quit as soon as they found better jobs. These men had passed
the examination and might have been hired as distribution clerks had
women not been hired for those jobs. Some women clerks quit because
they must lift eighty-pound sacks; some do the lifting and run the risk
of injury; some ask a man to help. When men do help, it not only
reduces efficiency but causes resentment. One supervisor said he had
noticed that the men who were first to jump to the women's assistance
were the ones who complained the loudest about the imposition.

According to the "Turnover Report," 19 percent of departing employees stated that one of their main reasons for leaving was the
home-study requirement for schemes that were seldom used. Although
new employees were told about the need for home study during their
preinduction interview, they were frequently surprised by the complexity of the schemes and the amount of home study required; they
regarded this requirement as a breach of their agreement. New employees often misunderstood the work involved, which had a bearing
on their propensity to quit: 693 of 3,678 such employees cited poor
working conditions, too-strenuous work, or dissatisfaction with
scheme requirements as reasons for quitting.[29]

The complexity of the schemes most clerks have to know has no
relation to their salary. Experienced clerks bid off assignments for
which they have been trained and give the more difficult schemes to
new employees. Increasing compensation for more difficult scheme
knowledge would probably decrease the turnover associated with
scheme clerks, and also reduce error rates.

Before reorganization, lack of opportunities for advancement
because of the political patronage system and local residence requirements accounted for some quits among postmasters and employees.
Typically a first-line supervisor waited from twelve to twenty years
for his promotion to postmaster. A ruling by the Civil Service Commission made it practically impossible to transfer postmasters from

[29] Post Office Department, *Internal Audit Report*, Review of Employees' Separation and Turnover, Phase II, January 1966 to May 1967, p. 62.

small post offices to larger ones, and this also dampened morale. Under Postal Service regulations promotions are supposed to be made on the basis of merit. However, employees still cannot transfer freely between one post office and another or between different crafts because, according to the terms of the national contracts between the Postal Service and the unions, there is a loss of seniority when such transfers occur.

Some substitute employees cited unpredictable and erratic work hours, insufficient take-home pay, and weekend work as major causes for quitting the Post Office. Because of the seniority system, newly hired employees are usually assigned to the least desirable positions under the least desirable conditions. Rookie mail handlers are assigned to the graveyard shift in the terminal; rookie scheme clerks get the most difficult schemes. Substitutes, who are not guaranteed a forty-hour work week, also complained about insufficient working time and low pay. They said that to approach forty hours of work a week they were often inconvenienced by having to work six days a week with ten- or twelve-hour shifts on some days and two- or three-hour shifts on others, and had to work weekends and holidays with no premium pay. The subs also complained that the youth employment program made it more difficult for them to work forty hours a week.

Regular permanent employees make their jobs pleasant and secure through the use of seniority privileges. They have been successful in influencing the rules and conditions of employment to enhance the nonpecuniary aspects of their jobs at the expense of newer substitute employees. Their demands were acceded to by Congress, which did not understand the consequences, by inadequately trained managers, and by top executives who had no reason to resist. The discrepancy in working conditions explains the difference in quit rates between regular and substitute postal workers.

Along with relative wages, the working conditions, seniority system, fringe benefits, job security, and other nonpecuniary advantages affecting the work atmosphere in the Postal Service have an important influence on the level of quits. For a technical discussion of these factors, the relationship between them, and their empirical counterparts used to estimate the parameters of the relationship, see Appendix A.

4

EVALUATING WAGES

Techniques for Evaluating Wages

Among the standards commonly applied to determine the appropriateness of wage levels are the "competitive theory of the labor market," the "prevailing wage standard," and the "cost of living principle."

"Competitive theory" suggests that in the labor market a given occupation in a given area under similar working conditions should command an equilibrium wage tending to be uniform in the area for workers of the same quality, and that this wage should be optimal. Wage surveys, however, report considerable and persistent differences in wage rates for a given job in different firms. In theory, the equilibrium wage should tend to prevail at all jobs as workers obtain information on the dispersion of wages and move from relatively low to relatively high-wage jobs. Labor market studies find, however, that workers seldom are knowledgeable about alternative positions or engage in systematic job searches. Consequently, some observers have concluded that the labor market is not competitive or that the theory is defective. This finding, however, makes scant allowance for variations in worker quality, for differences in working conditions, or for movement of relative demands for labor. These variables, among others, make it difficult if not impossible to use the theoretical standard of a uniform wage within a homogeneous labor market as the test for optimal wages in either the private or the public sector.[1]

There are inevitable difficulties in setting wages for government employees because in most cases the output does not pass through

---

[1] Walter Fogle and David Lewin, "Public Sector Wage Determination," Research Paper No. 30 (N.Y.: Columbia University, Graduate School of Business, 1974), p. 7.

the market where its relative worth is assessed by customers. Managers do not hold their jobs at the pleasure of stockholders who are interested in the efficiency of the operations. In the absence of this discipline, managers of public enterprises lack both a market standard for wages and the incentive to pay the optimal wage to maintain efficiency.

The "prevailing wage standard" as used by the Tennessee Valley Authority Act prescribes ". . . that no less than the prevailing rate of wages for work of a similar nature prevailing in the vicinity shall be paid to such laborers or mechanics." The TVA Act is perhaps the most explicit effort to use the prevailing wage standard for government employees. However, the words *prevail* and *vicinity* are not defined by law, making it the responsibility of labor and management to interpret the specific wage facts. The working definition of vicinity has gradually expanded until it includes the entire watershed of the Tennessee River and adjacent major urban areas such as Birmingham, Louisville, and Atlanta. As a prelude to negotiation, labor and management annually conduct a wage survey to obtain data on the wages that "prevail." For the wages of operating and maintenance workers, some seventy-two companies jointly selected by TVA and labor representatives are surveyed. For the wages of construction workers, data are collected from local unions, construction contractors, and contractor associations in fourteen cities. Discrepancies in the data are resolved by a joint committee prior to negotiations. The single rate that TVA will ultimately pay for a given class of work lies somewhere between the lowest and the highest rate found to "prevail." No mathematical formulas are applied. The rate is determined by bargaining according to: (1) the number working at a given rate; (2) the proximity of the rate surveyed to the principal center or centers of TVA operations; (3) comparability of jobs surveyed with jobs in TVA; and (4) unwritten equities that both TVA and labor deem important in order to maintain a satisfactory wage structure.

The "prevailing wage standard" is also the basis of the pay scales determined by the Federal Wage Board for blue-collar workers in federal employment, and by the telephone system for certain workers, although modified somewhat by cost-of-living considerations. As a prelude to a stronger reliance on the "prevailing wage standard," the Postal Service labor agreement in 1973 called for a new job evaluation program for supervisory management and noncraft employees to peg pay at the levels paid for comparable work in the private sector.[2]

---

[2] *Annual Report of the Postmaster General, 1972-73*, p. 19.

On the surface, paying government employees the equivalent of private industry wages seems to be a satisfactory principle. On closer examination, however, the application of this rule is not simple and is certainly not fair for all employees. Consider, for instance, the wide range of wages paid for most private-sector jobs, the anomalous wage rates established under union or corporate power, the complex nature of employment compensation, and the absence of a private market for some government occupations: all cause severe problems in applying the "prevailing wage standard."[3]

The wage range alone poses almost insurmountable problems because wages for less well-defined occupations like clerk or laborer vary as much as 100 percent in a given market. The spread of tasks assigned to these occupations may also vary widely within a community, making the determination of a prevailing wage even more imprecise.

Labor markets influenced by such noncompetitive forces as union or corporate pressure tend to offer wages significantly above or below the levels prevailing in a competitive market. The policy of surveying wages only in large firms and other government agencies engaging in comparable work significantly overstates general wage levels.[4] If a dispute persists over the "prevailing" wages, the question may be referred to the secretary of labor for determination and decision. When wages are decided in this manner, the prevailing wage rule is not reliable.

Public agencies in general take into account neither the complex nonwage aspects of public employment compensation (job security, pension plans, and lack of pressure) nor the unfavorable aspects of private employment that affect market wages. The government generally offers attractive fringe benefits and more stable employment than most private employers.[5] Failure to consider these can produce wage rates in the public sector that are higher than necessary to attract a work force, hence excessive. Given the range of discretion in decision making, the political processes exemplified by TVA negotiations also tend to set excessive wage rates for government jobs.[6]

For these reasons the prevailing-wage rule is unsatisfactory for evaluating wages and will not be used in this study. The evaluation of wage rates in terms of the "prevailing wage standard" is particularly

---

[3] Fogle and Lewin, "Public Sector Wage Determination," p. 6.

[4] Ibid., p. 12.

[5] Ibid., p. 19.

[6] Ibid., p. 7.

difficult for the Postal Service because most of the functions performed by its workers have unique aspects.

Industries with high proportions of skilled manpower and high marginal productivity of labor tend to pass along their higher wage levels to their semiskilled and unskilled occupations. On the other hand, wages for semiskilled and unskilled workers in the service and trade industries are substantially lower than in the high productivity industries. Wage rates in the Postal Service for unskilled and semiskilled labor, the pool from which the Postal Service recruits most of its workers, tend to be in the upper range of prevailing wage rates.

As noted, the level of Postal Service entry wages is usually very competitive. Even in metropolitan areas where semiskilled and unskilled workers are much in demand, the Postal Service attracts large numbers of applicants. There have been few instances where the Postal Service has not been able to meet its manpower needs. In 1966-1967, when some recruitment difficulties were reported, the Post Office was engaged in the largest percentage increase in employment since 1950.[7]

The cost-of-living principle is a means of introducing wage differentials for the same job performed in different parts of the country. The object is for workers performing the same task to receive the same real wage, that is, the nominal wage divided by a local cost-of-living index. This principle has neither the simplicity of the uniform money wage nor the market justification of the prevailing wage. Comparable cost-of-living indexes are difficult to determine except in the principal metropolitan areas where the data are regularly collected. The cost-of-living principle can be used to assign differentials to different areas, but it must be added to a base figure established by another means.

The Specific Human Capital Model

The specific human capital model is used in this study to evaluate wages. "Specific" refers to occupational skills needed by one employer in particular. Training that is mainly suited to the firms providing it is called specific training. "Nonspecific" human capital comprises those skills useful to employers in general. Rational firms pay employees with general training the same wage they could get elsewhere. There is little concern about turnover because the cost of the training is

---

[7] Kappel Commission, *Towards Postal Excellence*, vol. 1, p. 34.

entirely borne by the employees.[8] Most training for jobs has both a specific and a general value.

The knowledge acquired by new employees in company indoctrination programs is a form of specific training. Other kinds of hiring costs, such as employment agency fees or the costs of interviewing, testing, checking references, and bookkeeping obviously do not increase the productivity of new employees elsewhere, and so are also a form of specific investment in human capital. These costs are an investment because they have an effect on productivity over time, and are specific because productivity is raised primarily in the firms making the outlays. They are in human capital because they lose their value when the employees leave.[9]

Specific human capital is embodied in the worker. The worker owns his skills once they are developed and they cannot be used without his permission. If a worker quits to take another job after he has been specifically trained, the capital expended on him is lost; no further returns can be collected. Likewise if a worker is fired after he himself has paid for specific training, he suffers a capital loss. Hence, a mutual interest exists between the worker and the company to share the cost and the returns of specific human capital. The larger the share of the cost borne by the employee, the less is his incentive to quit and the safer is the employer's share of the cost. It is therefore in the employer's interest to have the employee share part of the cost and returns from specific human capital. However, the employee will not be willing to bear the whole cost without employment guarantees that ensure the safety and yield of his investment.[10] Consequently, he will insist that the firm also bear part of the cost of augmenting his specific human capital.

Postal Service regulars are very secure in their positions. A postal regular cannot be discharged from the service except "for cause" and enjoys virtually continuous tenure. He may remain as long as he likes in a position and may not be transferred to another post office or craft against his will. His wage rate is unaffected whether he works four or forty hours a week. This type of job security acts as an inducement for the Postal Service regular to invest some of his resources into his specific human capital.[11] One way he does this is by accepting a re-

---

[8] Gary S. Becker, *Human Capital* (New York: Columbia University Press, 1964), p. 24.

[9] Becker, *Human Capital*, p. 19.

[10] Lester G. Telser, *Competition, Collusion and Game Theory* (Chicago: Aldine Atherton, 1972), pp. 315-16, 343, 349.

[11] Baratz, *The Economics of the Postal Service*, p. 27.

duced wage during the training period. However, postal workers have little incentive to continue this training beyond a certain minimum since promotions are made on the basis of seniority, not merit. Rational firms, on the other hand, pay a specifically trained employee a higher wage than he could get elsewhere because they are concerned about their own capital loss should the employee leave.[12]

Turnover takes its importance from the costs of specific training borne by workers or firms. If a worker with specific training quits, a new employee has to be hired whose productivity is less than the one who left. Training can raise the new worker's productivity too, but not without additional training costs and the loss due to the worker's temporary underproductivity. A firm is hurt by the departure of trained employees because an equally productive new employee cannot be readily found.[13] Taking these factors into account, one would expect the value of specific human capital per worker to be inversely related to the quit rate.[14]

Once a firm has invested in training one of its employees, it has several means of persuading the employee to remain. These include the offer of higher wages, more regular employment, pensions, fringe benefits, and deferred compensation. The firm recoups its investment in specific human capital by obtaining a marginal product from the worker over the expected tenure of his employment that exceeds the wage.[15]

In a short-run theory of employment, labor can be regarded as a quasi-fixed factor, meaning that total labor costs are partially variable and partially fixed. The fixed costs are the investment in specific human capital incurred in hiring, training, and raising workers to full productivity. The costs are fixed in the sense that they have already been expended on the labor force. Such costs, usually called personnel costs, can be separated into hiring and training costs. Hiring costs include recruiting, processing, and setting up payroll and personnel records. Training expenses are investments in the human agent designed to improve a worker's productivity on the job. The gains from a lower quit rate are greater for firms having workers possessing a greater value of specific human capital.

The largest part of total labor costs is the wages bill, which is variable, representing payments for a flow of productive services. By increasing the wage rate, a firm can reduce the number of workers

[12] Becker, *Human Capital*, pp. 18, 24.
[13] Ibid., pp. 21-22.
[14] Telser, *Competition*, pp. 315-16, 340.
[15] Ibid., p. 340.

who quit, thereby saving on personnel costs, but increasing payroll costs. An efficient firm will choose a wage that minimizes total personnel costs and the wages bill. This wage is considered to be the optimal wage. The mathematical expression for the optimal wage rate that minimizes the total labor costs of a firm is detailed in Appendix A.

By using the expression for the relationship between the quit and wage rates discussed in chapter 3, and the equation relating total labor costs to personnel costs and wage costs, the optimal wage rate can be calculated as a function of the quit and wage rates in all manufacturing, the parameters of the quit–wage rate relationship, and the average personnel costs associated with hiring a new recruit. The value of personnel costs associated with a new recruit for the Postal Service is estimated in chapter 5, after which the numerical values of the optimal wage can be calculated and used to evaluate wages paid Postal Service employees.

5

THE ESTIMATION
OF PERSONNEL COSTS

For the purpose of this study it is important to know the cost of replacing employees who quit. Whether it is worthwhile for an employer to increase wage rates in order to reduce quits depends upon the cost of replacing quits. Accordingly, one might think that there would be a wealth of published information about replacement costs in business; but this is not so. Part of the reason for this is that in a given firm the necessary data are generally spread across several departments, any or all of which withhold information that might be damaging to them. For instance, the cost of interviewing applicants, exit interviews, and other personnel functions may be in the personnel department, while training costs for the new employees may be the responsibility of the training section or the shop foreman.

Company departments are generally reluctant to supply to top managers information about increased accident or production costs caused by new employees, because this places them in an unfavorable light.[1] Personnel employees also have a strong incentive not to report the cost of labor turnover because management generally regards turnover as wasteful and avoidable. Department managers would jeopardize their own positions by volunteering figures showing problematic turnover costs.[2] Even if department heads cooperate in gathering turnover data there are difficulties in making cost calculations. Many expenses must be imputed, including the cost of interviewing time spent by employees other than those in the personnel department, training costs, productivity losses during the training period, and the costs of spoilage and extra supervision.

---

[1] Gaudet, *Labor Turnover*, p. 12.

[2] Ibid., pp. 8 and 12.

The variability in the cost of filling positions increases the difficulty in making estimates. An ideal applicant may walk into the personnel office the day the requisition is approved or the position may be filled only after an expensive search. Costs also vary directly with the tightness of the labor market. In a tight market new hires are more expensive to recruit because they require more screening and training and are more likely to quit sooner. Costs vary with the urgency of filling a vacancy. If it is important to fill the position without delay, expensive methods of recruitment are used; if more time can be spent searching, the cost will be lower. For these reasons good estimates of turnover costs are hard to find.

Company policies may have a significant impact on turnover. For instance, imposing high performance standards for employees might lead to high levels of productivity but could also produce a high quit rate. When management has accurate information it can calculate the length of time an employee must work in a specified position before it can recover the specific human capital invested in him. In many firms, the costly fringe benefits that accrue after seniority of a specific period would have to be taken into account. No sound personnel decisions affecting quits can be made until the full cost to the company of losing an employee is balanced against the full costs of keeping him.[3]

Many company policies other than adjusting wages influence turnover, including selection techniques, training methods, recruitment, and supervision. A firm should increase its expenditures on its total personnel program until the last dollar spent just contributes an extra dollar saved through increased productivity or a lower quit rate. For the same reason, within the total personnel program the expenditures should be allocated among the different programs until the last dollar spent on each program reduces the costs of producing any given output by one dollar. When these conditions have been established, personnel expenditures for the firm will be optimal.

One fruit of investment in training is neglected in the analysis used here to determine the optimal wage, namely that increasing the productivity of workers through a training program reduces the number of workers required to perform the same amount of work. The model used in this study does not treat the labor force as a variable and so does not permit measuring the effect of training on the productivity and size of the work force, except as these are reflected in personnel costs. To estimate the optimal wage level for the Post Office

---

[3] Ibid., p. 38.

and Postal Service it is sufficient to take the personnel costs per new recruit as given. In the more general model proposed in Appendix A, personnel costs would be treated as a function of many variables, and an optimal level of personnel costs for a particular industry could be calculated simultaneously with optimal wage and quit rates. A review of the literature on personnel costs with some estimates for industries other than the Postal Service is found in Appendix B.

Hiring in the Postal Service

In the late 1960s the Post Office was hiring approximately 150,000 workers annually. New hires fell during the early 1970s because Postmaster General Klassen, anticipating large productivity gains after reorganization, put a freeze on hiring to reduce the work force by 50,000 employees. The new efficiencies were not realized, however, and hiring was sharply increased after a breakdown in service in December 1973. When the number of postal employees is growing, new appointments of 200,000 annually are not unusual. Recruitment is seldom difficult except in some of the larger cities. For instance, in some suburbs north and west of Chicago, where living standards were high, the Postal Service had a problem attracting recruits. However, not all available recruiting procedures were utilized. For instance, there was no recruiting at military discharge centers, which are likely places to find prospective applicants. Form 2415, "An Important Message from Your Postmaster," which proved to be very effective in producing applicants elsewhere, was not used. This form, which advertises jobs in the Postal Service, could be delivered to every household served by a post office. It generally produces a barrage of applicants. When Form 2415 was distributed in one zone in Chicago it produced such a sudden flux of applicants that it was not used again. Brooklyn did not use Form 2415, nor did the city of Detroit; however, it was used effectively in the Detroit suburbs. Better qualified employees were chosen out of the numerous applicants responding to Form 2415.[4]

In the recruitment and hiring process before the reorganization, the postmaster first requested the Civil Service Commission to schedule and conduct an examination to establish a register of eligible applicants. This took two to three weeks. Since the exams are offered only when there are recruiting needs, the application rate in many locations offers no useful information on the size of the application queue. In large cities, where the examination is offered daily or several times a

---

[4] Post Office Department, *Internal Audit Report*, p. 46.

week, the practice of offering the exam only on weekdays, when employees working elsewhere find it difficult to attend, reduces the number of applications. Scoring the examination took an additional week or more. This was followed by a review of the individual applicants to determine suitability and qualifications. A delay in the reply from one reference of a single applicant can hold up the processing of the entire list of applicants. An arrest, health, and prior work record check took another two weeks. Applicants were allowed ten days to reply to follow-up inquiries by the Civil Service Commission, after which the register was forwarded to the postmaster within three days. Applicants were then asked if they were available for employment. The postmaster interviewed the top three candidates for each vacancy before making his choice. Offering a position to the chosen applicant generally took another three weeks.[5]

These cumbersome procedures have not changed substantially since reorganization. To gain an appreciation for how Post Office/Postal Service recruitment procedures camouflage the size of the applicant queue, in fiscal 1967 1.5 million applicants for employment were received by the Post Office; 840,000, or 56 percent of applicants, took the examination; 405,000 passed the exam and became eligible; and of these, 178,000 accepted employment. In New York City, a total of 34,191 applications were filed in response to the announcement of positions available. However, only 17,937 sat for the examination and 4,335, or 24.1 percent, passed.[6] Many qualified job seekers obtained positions elsewhere before being reached for an interview. The length of time taken to process the applications and offer jobs was responsible for the low acceptance rate among eligibles. When it took over thirteen weeks to hire an employee in fiscal 1967, 67 percent of the job applicants in seventeen large metropolitan areas did not wait around to complete the process. In fiscal 1967, the job acceptance rate for temporaries in the clerk or carrier crafts was as low as 10 percent in some cities.[7]

Prompt offers to applicants, as in private industry, would seem to be essential to sound recruitment. In areas where recruitment is difficult, even a few days delay between examination and an offer of appointment would probably reduce the job acceptance rate. In the most difficult areas, like the suburbs of Chicago and Detroit where the registers are exhausted, temporary appointments to the Postal Service have been approved. This permits a job offer with no delay and fre-

---

[5] Kappel Commission, *Towards Postal Excellence*, vol. 5, p. 105.

[6] Post Office Department, *Internal Audit Report*, p. 48.

[7] Kappel Commission, *Towards Postal Excellence*, vol. 1, p. 104.

quently obtains satisfactory employees. In past practice, the unattractiveness of the initial Post Office job offered—usually a temporary or substitute position—also contributed to the low acceptance rate. This may still be the case in the Postal Service.

The high percentage of eligibles lost before appointment multiplies average recruitment costs per new hire. A large portion of personnel offices' budgets must be spent to process paper work for applicants who are never hired.

Orientation and training programs developed by individual post offices involves considerable duplication of effort, are not uniform, and are often of questionable value. Orientation programs initiated by the post offices for the reception, induction, and adjustment of new employees to their work environment include all of the topics required by the *Postal Service Manual*, but the depth of the coverage varies significantly. For instance, preemployment interviews were not always conducted in all post offices. In the Chicago south suburban office preemployment interviews were conducted with only some of the new hires. In Baltimore, Richmond, and Washington, the personnel interview was conducted after applicants were hired. Some offices did not use preemployment interviews but relied on the use of forms. The presentations in interviews were generally not interesting and used words like *schemes, annual leave,* and *casing mail* that were probably not understood by the applicants. A preemployment interview usually emphasized adverse working conditions and important work disciplinary rules more than employee benefits. Such interviews must have reduced the hire rate.

Since reorganization, the Postal Service conducts the testing, scoring, and eventual hiring of employees, but under the same rules and procedures used earlier by the Civil Service Commission. The tests also remain the same, and although they are now marked by computer at the National Testing and Scoring Center in Los Angeles, they still take three weeks to mark and return.

Not only is the acceptance rate of jobs offered to eligibles low in the Postal Service, but also among these same newly hired employees turnover is much higher than for longer term employees.[8] Too high a turnover rate among new employees reduces the efficiency of the overall operation. Usually new employees enter the Postal Service as career

---

[8] While the annual quit rate for all postal employees has varied between 4.75 and 13.42 percent between 1958 and 1976, the quit rate for career regulars has been quite stable at about 1.8 percent—perhaps varying at the most 1 percentage point in either direction. (Source: J. G. Tiedemann, Personnel Research Division, U.S. Postal Service.)

substitutes. While a substitute, the employee must be available for call, but he has no assurance of any fixed amount of employment. If called to work, he is guaranteed at least two hours of employment that day. In smaller post offices it may be many years before the substitute succeeds to a regular or full-time position. During this period he works irregular hours, goes without steady employment, and lives on hope until he receives a regular appointment. Obviously, these unpleasant conditions make postal employment for newly hired employees less than attractive. The elimination of the present classification of temporary employees and improved working schedules for career substitutes—the two employee groups that account for most of the turnover—would reduce the turnover rate of newly hired employees.

If postal workers are overpaid there would be a tendency for quits to be lower than optimal and for the number of qualified applicants to be large relative to the number of openings available. In the absence of offsetting policies one would expect to find a long queue of workers seeking jobs in the Postal Service. This would be an embarrassing demonstration of excessive wages. The number of applicants for postal jobs is, however, effectively camouflaged by two personnel devices, namely, the examination system and the division of workers into two groups. No employees are hired without an examination, and the examinations are given at the pleasure of the local post office only when there is a need for employees. By scheduling the examination on weekdays rather than on weekends the number of applicants available to write the exam is reduced. The long delay between the exams and actual hiring also tends to reduce the size of the queue.

The turnover problem is further concealed by the fact that newly hired employees receive the most unpleasant jobs, irregular working hours, and disagreeable work schedules. This arrangement is almost like an initiation ordeal. The postal workers with seniority benefit from it because it enhances the value of their jobs; the arrangement also spares management from an even more embarrasingly low turnover rate because it encourages turnover among the newly hired workers.

Reorganization abolished the practice of political appointments in the Postal Service but left most other hiring procedures untouched. Apparently the creation of the Postal Service as a government corporation has not provided the incentive to reform such procedures. The vested interests of regular workers are still enhanced by these cumbersome hiring procedures and seniority rules, at the expense of overall efficiency.

Training in the Postal Service

New workers require time and training to achieve the level of productivity of the employees they replace. According to Postal Service sources, six months to a year are necessary for most new employees to reach a satisfactory level of performance, yet the highest rate of turnover occurs among employees within this period. Turnover in the Postal Service implies lower productivity not only among new workers but also among more senior employees because of existing personnel practices. That is, the turnover often necessitates multiple shifts among existing employees to jobs demanding new scheme knowledge in which they will be less productive.

As a part of their orientation programs, post offices distribute to new employees the Code of Ethical Conduct, the *ZIP Code Directory*, and other materials explaining such matters as leave, attendance, lunch periods, sanctity of the mails, and personal habits. It is unlikely, however, that this is sufficient to prepare the worker to assume the full responsibilities of his job.

A new employee must learn the procedures for handling mail, postal organization, the details of his own and others' jobs, civil defense, safety, and many other subjects. Much of this knowledge must be acquired on the employee's own time, a policy contributing to turnover among newly hired employees. Though clerks must qualify and requalify to hold their positions, they are not paid for the time spent in mastering schemes nor compensated according to the extent and complexity of their scheme knowledge. Postal turnover is increased when scheme clerks either fail to learn schemes or refuse to learn schemes seldom used because of ZIP coding.

There were and are wide variations in the quality and quantity of training provided at different postal installations. In installations with 500 employees or more, regulations authorize a training officer to present lectures, films, demonstrations, and other forms of instruction. Installations without training officers have no organized instruction and can give only on-the-job training to the newly hired or newly promoted employees. In these cases the amount, nature, and quality of training depend on the inclinations of the postmaster. Even if the postmaster is favorably disposed toward improving training he is restricted in the amount of time he can allow as well as in the personnel he can assign to the task. At some larger installations postmasters maintain vacancies at a certain level so they can invest the man-hours made available in training. This procedure is insufficient to maintain comprehensive training programs, however; only the most elementary needs can be met and then only if there are no unexpected increases in work load. For scheme employees, training of up to thirty hours of official work time is authorized by the regional manual but some of the large offices were not providing any training at all while others limit the training because of manpower budget requirements. Low postal productivity is almost certainly related to the small amount of training Postal Service employees are given.

The Kappel Report criticized at length the meager and ineffective training programs in the Post Office and suggested many reforms. Since reorganization the Postal Service has improved its training programs. The present training system includes a national network of 200 postal employee development centers which offer seventy job-related curricula in most large post offices to assist employees in the development of their postal careers. Employees receive training in mathematics and electricity in addition to postal skills. At the Technical Center of the Training and Development Institute in Norman, Oklahoma, maintenance men receive training in the operation and repair of complicated postal machinery. Nearly 22,000 postmasters, supervisors, and other managers received training at the Postal Service Training and Development Institute in Bethesda, Maryland, and at five regional field centers during fiscal year 1973. Some 500,000 postal employees during the year were involved in home-study courses on service standards, courtesy to the public, parcel post damage reduction, and operation of sorting machines.[9] The Executive Development Program, which typically chooses ten managers with executive potential and sends them to a leading university, was curtailed in fiscal year 1976 and scheduled to resume in fiscal year 1977. Despite this new emphasis on training, the amount spent on training per employee per year is still small and gains in productivity have not been noticeable.

Personnel Cost Estimates for the Postal Service

An estimate of a portion of the training cost per new postal employee can be made from the *National Payroll Hours Summary Report* for the fiscal year June 26, 1971, to June 23, 1972. During this period the on-the-clock training costs, including the wages paid to employees conducting the training and to the trainee, was $20,849,601. Average employment in the Postal Service over the period was 700,000 and the average turnover rate was 15 percent. This computes to approximately 105,000 new employees hired and presumably trained during this pe-

---

[9] *Annual Report of the Postmaster General, 1972-1973*, pp. 20, 22.

riod. Since the new employees were the primary beneficiaries of the training costs, this indicates a training cost of about $200 per new employee.[10]

The highest training costs are for scheme distributors and particularly for incoming rather than outgoing distributors. Incoming distributors in large cities are required to learn four incoming primary schemes as well as one or two incoming secondary schemes. It takes approximately one full year for a clerk to learn his incoming schemes. On outgoing schemes distribution practice is usually not given until the clerk qualifies on all sections of his scheme exam. The opinion of operating personnel queried is that it would take up to one year for a clerk to become proficient on outgoing schemes. Cost information on administering the scheme-training program is not available, but the cost is believed to be substantial. A portion of the cost of scheme administration is imputable to the large percentage of clerks who are separated for scheme failure (21 percent based on the turnover study) and a probable large percentage who separate before reaching a point of adverse action for scheme failure.[11]

Perhaps the largest cost associated with turnover is the drop in production caused by the loss of employees, particularly the loss of trained scheme distributors, and the excessive overtime at the post offices where there is difficulty in replacing separated scheme employees. The cost of underproduction of new employees is difficult to measure; other than in scheme work, however, it is thought to be nominal because a new employee can become reasonably efficient in a few days. The distribution clerks do not reach peak efficiency until two years after they start learning schemes. In addition to increased costs due to slowed scheme distribution, the use of partially trained clerks increases the quantity of misdirected mail.[12] The Bureau of Operations has stated that offices with a shortage of scheme distributors will often have a very high distribution error rate, *with rates of 25 percent not being uncommon*. This involves double handling of mail and obviously increased costs.

Employees with less than one year of service have a higher accident rate than senior employees in their craft. Employees with less than one year represented 20.95 percent of the average work force but had 33.76 percent of all accidents in fiscal year 1966. Employees with more than one year, representing 79.05 percent of the average comple-

---

[10] U.S. Postal Service, *National Payroll Hours Summary Report*, Report for Fiscal Year June 26, 1971, to June 23, 1972.

[11] Post Office Department, *Internal Audit Report*, pp. 41 and 44.

[12] Ibid., p. 8.

ment, had 66.24 percent of all accidents. These figures were developed by the Cost Analysis Division, Bureau of Finance and Administration. Its study was based on an analysis of supervisors' accident reports (Form 1278) for fiscal year 1966 in eight large offices having a total of 94,349 employees.[13] The extra cost of the accident proneness of new employees for fiscal year 1966 was approximately $3.5 million.[14]

The most important item in turnover cost, which has not been measured, is the loss from decreased productivity. Eighty percent of postal employees are clerks, carriers, and mail handlers. The rest are supervisors, managers, and a few technical specialists. It is reported that to bring a mail handler up to minimum standards of productivity takes approximately one week; for a clerk who sorts mail six weeks; for a carrier who has to learn his route approximately three weeks. These are the times generally required to reach *minimum standards*. If an employee stays with the post office for eighteen-to-twenty-four months, the Postal Service feels that it recoups its investment in training and other personnel costs.[15] The substitute employee may be trained for a number of different jobs. Under Post Office procedures, because of the rotation of substitute carriers, it was believed that a carrier could not reach peak efficiency until he had established a route. A Post Office Department study showed that all measures of productivity increased with length of tenure, especially in the first year or two.[16] The excessive overtime at post offices where separated employees cannot be easily replaced is also an on-the-job cost of turnover. In the Chicago area there were eleven suburban post offices that used more than 10 hours of overtime for each 100 hours straight time during November 1966. At one office the rate was 29.5 percent.[17]

Part of the on-the-job costs are uniforms for newly hired workers. Eligible new employees receive from $67 to $175 for uniforms, depending on their job and the type of uniform required.[18]

The Internal Audit Division and the Cost Analysis Division, Bureau of Finance and Administration, have made exploratory studies

[13] Kappel Commission, *Towards Postal Excellence*, vol. 4, p. 5.189.

[14] Post Office Department, *Internal Audit Report*, p. 40.

[15] Dr. J. G. Tiedemann, Personnel Research Division (unpublished study), 1967.

[16] Kappel Commission, *Towards Postal Excellence*, vol. 3, p. 2.28.

[17] Post Office Department, *Internal Audit Report*, p. 8.

[18] Agreement between the U.S. Postal Service and American Postal Workers Union, AFL-CIO; National Association of Letter Carriers, AFL-CIO; National Post Office Mail Handlers, Watchmen, Messengers and Group Leaders, Division of Labor, International Union of North America, AFL-CIO; National Rural Letter Carriers Association, July 21, 1973, to July 20, 1975, p. 41.

into the cost of employee turnover. For calendar year 1966, to replace the 147,101 separations, the costs were as follows:[19]

Recruitment	$ 6,207,662
Separation	1,284,192
Training	5,148,535
Accident proneness of new employees	3,512,081
Total	$16,152,470

The training hours reported were incomplete in detail, so the cost for training and developing a postal employee could not be reliably calculated.

In July 1967 the Cost Analysis Division, Bureau of Finance and Administration, completed a profile study of first-year employees. J. G. Tiedemann of the Personnel Research Division reported that in this study the average personnel costs for recruiting, testing, hiring, training (with the attendant loss in productivity), and the eventual termination were found to be approximately $2,000 per new employee. This suggests an annual turnover cost approaching $300 million. In some areas of the country turnover costs might have been as high as $2,500; in others perhaps as low as $1,500. Such costs depend on the elaborateness of the personnel programs (which are usually run with considerable fixed costs) and the number of new employees processed within the time period. Post Office personnel costs varied between small towns and large cities and depended on the kind of training program in existence. Large city post offices tended to have more elaborate programs while those in rural areas usually had none. If a post office had an elaborate program, it also had certain fixed costs associated with the program. If the post office was not processing many new applicants the average training costs per employee would have been relatively higher during this period. This phenomenon accounts for some of the variation in the personnel costs between areas in the United States.

I have chosen three estimates of the personnel costs per new employee in 1972: $1,500, $2,000, and $2,500.[20] In so doing I have leaned

---

[19] Post Office Department, *Internal Audit Report*, p. 38.

[20] This study does not wish to build the inefficiencies of the Postal Service's personnel program into the model for evaluating wages. The $2,000 cost per new recruit in 1967 is inflated because of the inefficient recruiting and work assignment policies and excessive wages. If for the moment we assume that personnel costs per new recruit were $2,000 in 1972 the wage evaluation model suggests that Post Office wages were excessive by approximately 20 percent in 1967. If this excess is deducted from the $2,000 it leaves a personnel cost figure

heavily on the results of the most recent Postal Service study. These figures are based chiefly on estimates provided by the Postal Service but also fall within the range of costs given by nine controllers who said the costs of replacing clerks were from $50 to $2,000, and $250 to $7,000 for clerks with higher skills.[21] These estimates are also consistent with the few studies available that estimate personnel costs, and with the knowledge we have of Postal Service personnel programs and operations.

---

of $1,600 per new recruit. However, inefficiencies in the structure and management of the personnel program have yet to be taken into account. It is easy to imagine additional efficiencies of this type accounting for savings of $150 per new recruit which would reduce the personnel costs to $1,450 in 1967.

Between 1967 and 1972 the postal budget and presumably the amount spent on personnel costs in the Post Office/Postal Service rose by 54 percent. Again to avoid building inefficiencies into the estimate of personnel costs the index of average hourly earnings was used to inflate the personnel costs figure rather than the postal budget. Using the index (which increased from 100 to 137.9 between 1967 and 1972) personnel costs per new recruit in 1972 would become $2,000.

[21] Gaudet, *Labor Turnover*, p. 11.

6

THE DETERMINATION
OF OPTIMAL WAGES

Introduction

In this chapter the amount of excessive wages paid Postal Service employees is calculated using the model described in chapters 3-5. The relative performance of the U.S. and foreign postal services is evaluated, and the results suggest that the U.S. Postal Service is less efficient. A comparison with the postal service in the United Kingdom in particular reveals that the most important source of inefficiency in the U.S. Postal Service is the excessive wages paid to its employees. Postal wages in this country are about 30 percent higher than those in the United Kingdom relative to the respective standards of living in the two countries. Sharon P. Smith, using the Becker-Mincer human capital model, finds that postal workers were overpaid in 1973 by 30 percent. Her estimates are consistent with the results of this study. Among the other findings of this study is that the breakdowns of postal services in Chicago in 1966 and 1970 may have been precipitated by a negative wage differential there.

Another objective of this chapter is to try to understand the conditions in the Postal Service that have made possible and even encouraged excessive wages. To this end we will consider some of the company policies and market characteristics that have led to excessive wages elsewhere and compare these with policies prevailing in the Postal Service. Henry Simons and Lester Telser suggest that excessive wages are paid more frequently when firms have some monopoly power. The Postal Service is a one-firm industry having an absolute monopoly over first-class mail. This circumstance makes it not only possible but altogether likely for the service to pay excessive wages. If low elasticity of demand for the services of a firm is regarded as a measure of the firm's ability to pay excessive wages and pass the extra cost on to the public, the Postal Service undoubtedly rates high in its ability to do so. While reliable estimates of the elasticity of demand for different types of mail are hard to obtain, those available agree that the demands for different types of mail service appear to be inelastic in the relevant ranges, especially the demand for first-class mail where the imposing barriers to entry exist.[1]

H. Gregg Lewis found that unionism was responsible for raising wages by as much as 42 percent in the bituminous coal industry and by 24 percent in the commercial air transportation industry.[2] While the results of my study do not pertain to the same groups examined by Lewis nor attribute the whole of excess wages to unionism, my estimates for the amounts of excess wages in a wide range of two-digit industries and in the Postal Service are comparable in magnitude with Lewis's results. The Postal Service appears to have strong unions that have been very successful in raising the wages of their members. The effect of their efforts to raise wages to the excessive levels calculated in this study is quite consistent with their power as indicated by other characteristics.

Several internal characteristics of the Postal Service may also be responsible for the excessive wage level, namely managerial policy, the "prevailing wage theory" as applied to Postal Service wages, and the wage determination process itself. Postal managers are disposed to pay high wages because they have no incentives to do otherwise. This policy is made possible by the Private Express Statutes. The prevailing wage theory, which is a guide to setting wage levels for government employees, is easily manipulated and has undoubtedly contributed to excessive wages insofar as it has been used in setting postal wages. Since those granting wage increases are not responsible for paying them, the wage-setting process itself tends to generate unduly generous wages for government employees, including postal workers.

Melvin Lurie describes the experience of the Boston Carmen's Union in gaining excessive wages from the Metropolitan Transit Authority and comes very close to describing unwittingly the scenario

---

[1] Dr. Bernard Sobin's study, used in a recent rate case, found that the elasticities of demand for classes of mail other than first class were also inelastic because their rates are kept artificially low with subsidies from first-class profits. Even so the U.P.S. has taken over half of the parcel business and even second-class mailers with all their privileges are experimenting with private delivery. See footnote 15 below for particulars. Postal elasticities are also discussed in U.S. Postal Rate Commission, *Opinion and Recommended Decision: Postal Rate and Fee Increases, 1975*, Docket R76-1, Appendix H.

[2] H. Gregg Lewis, *Unionism and Relative Wages in the United States* (Chicago: University of Chicago Press), 1963, p. 280.

of the postal unions in achieving the same benefits from the Post Office/Postal Service. Both the MTA and the Post Office/Postal Service were faced with inelastic demands for their services, which allowed them to raise their rates and increase their revenues while enjoying the safety of monopoly protection from would-be entrants. Both achieved access to public funds to finance deficits, had strong unions to push for wage increases, and weak managers with little incentive to resist. When faced with an arbitration process, the Carmen's Union learned how to manipulate it to its own advantage. The process for settling disputes in the Postal Service since reorganization has not been tested yet. Faced with these situations it is little wonder that both unions were successful over long periods of time and under differing circumstances in gaining excessive wages for their members.

A Presentation of Results

I have calculated the optimal wages for the Post Office and the Postal Service from the specific human capital model discussed in chapter 4. The technical details are presented in Appendix A. The calculated optimal wages are listed together with the actual wages in Table 19.

Table 19

WAGES IN THE POST OFFICE AND POSTAL SERVICE

Year	Actual Average Hourly Wages	Optimal[a] Wages	Wage Excess (percent)
1958	$2.39	$1.61	32.8
1959	2.40	1.81	24.5
1960	2.41	1.79	25.8
1961	2.63	1.78	32.1
1962	2.62	1.91	26.9
1963	2.85	1.96	31.2
1964	2.92	2.05	29.8
1965	3.08	2.26	26.7
1966	3.19	2.57	19.4
1967	3.26	2.57	21.2
1968	3.44	2.68	22.2
1969	3.64	2.89	20.6
1970	4.03	2.85	29.3
1971	4.51	2.88	36.1
1972	4.79	3.23	32.6

a Optimal wages are calculated using an average personnel cost per new recruit of $2,000 in 1972.
Source: Tables A-4 and A-6 in Appendix A.

It may be seen that workers in the Postal Service were overpaid by 32.6 percent in 1972, which was more than for any two-digit industry considered (see Appendix A). Over the years 1958-1972, the mean excess postal wage was 27.4 percent, which ranked third highest among two-digit industries considered. These estimates at first might seem high. As indicated by the quit–wage rate relationship estimated in Appendix A, postal workers are neither much influenced by non-pecuniary aspects of their employment nor wage differentials between what they receive in the Postal Service and alternative opportunities elsewhere. Because of these two aspects of postal worker response, the Postal Service is not required to pay its workers as much as it does for purposes of efficiency, even though the average personnel cost per new recruit is $2,000. The evidence produced in this study indicates that postal workers are overpaid by approximately *one-third*. What, however, are the findings of others?

The Becker-Mincer Human Capital Model

Sharon P. Smith examined wages in the Postal Service using the Becker-Mincer human capital model and data from the May 1973 current-population-survey tape.[3] Her regression model has as its dependent variable the natural logarithm of the hourly wage rate estimated from the reported average weekly earnings and hours worked. The explanatory variables include education, experience, marital status, race, veteran status, size of urban area, geographic region, occupational group, regular or part-time status, dual-job status, union status, and sector of employment. A dummy variable was used to separate postal workers from the labor force overall and hence to measure the advantage accruing to them in the Postal Service.

Smith finds that both male and female postal workers have significantly higher wages than nonunionized, and at least comparable wages to unionized, private sector workers of similar socioeconomic characteristics. The average hourly wages for unionized postal workers were 58 percent higher for females and 26 percent higher for males than for nonunion workers in the private sector.[4] According to June 1972 figures, 18.6 percent of postal employees were female and 81.4

---

[3] Sharon P. Smith, "Wages in the Postal Service," Working Paper No. 68 (Princeton: Princeton University, Industrial Relations Section, April 1975). See also Jacob Mincer, *Schooling, Experience and Earnings* (New York: National Bureau of Economic Research, 1974).

[4] Smith finds that the wage advantage of unionized over nonunionized postal workers is insignificant.

percent male. Using these percentages as weights, Smith's differentials indicate that, overall, postal employees are overpaid by 31 percent. This estimate is remarkably close to the estimates developed in this study, which indicate that on average Postal Service workers were overpaid between 28 percent and 35 percent in 1972 depending on the estimate for average personnel costs.

There are several difficulties in applying the Becker-Mincer model to the Postal Service. The estimate derived from this model is based only on wage rates and does not take into account differences in fringe benefits, stability of employment, or intensity of work effort. But the nonpecuniary aspects of employment in the Postal Service are very important considerations to postal employees. A relatively few postal quits, in comparison with the other industries surveyed, occur for reasons associated with the nonpecuniary aspects of employment. The quit rate in the Postal Service, while very low, relative to other two-digit industries, is heavily influenced by the phase of the business cycle. In evaluating Postal Service wages the present study incorporates this information while the Smith study does not.

The Smith study uses primarily personal characteristics of the labor force and compares what workers of the same type would be likely to receive with different employers under different circumstances. Smith enters values for the personal and socioeconomic characteristics of a postal worker into the model and if the wage predicted is the same as what a similar worker would receive elsewhere, the postal wage is judged not to be excessive. This assumes that wages prevailing elsewhere for similar workers are optimal and that postal workers are not overqualified, which may not necessarily be true.

Despite the apparent difficulties with the Becker-Mincer model, the Smith estimates are remarkably close to those made in this study.

A Comparison of the Postal Service with Foreign Post Offices

A study examining the postal services in Belgium, Denmark, France, the Netherlands, Norway, Sweden, Switzerland, West Germany, Australia, Canada, New Zealand, Ireland, Great Britain, and the United States concluded that a higher degree of business orientation existed among foreign postal services than in the United States.[5] Such comparisons are difficult because in the United Kingdom (as in most European countries) the postal service is also responsible for telegraphs and telephones whereas in the United States these are run by separate enterprises.

---

[5] Kappel Commission, *Towards Postal Excellence*, vol. 5, p. 183.

In contrast to the all-but-inevitable annual Postal Service deficit, the United Kingdom did not suffer a loss on its postal services until 1962-1965; and since then not until 1972-1973. Since 1925 the U.S. Post Office/Postal Service has made a profit only in the three war years, 1943-1945. Relative wages paid postal employees in the two countries explain much of this difference.[6] The U.S. postman received an average of $5,300 a year in 1962 while his British counterpart received only $1,531. This difference was much greater than the difference in average income between the two countries. Average per capita income that year was $2,479 in the United States, and $1,206 in the United Kingdom. Average income in the United States was thus about twice the average income in the United Kingdom but postal salaries in the United States were three and one-half times postal salaries in the United Kingdom.[7]

These figures seem to suggest that the productivity of the average American postman in 1962 relative to other American workers was higher than the relative productivity of his British counterpart.[8] However, for a total expenditure eight times that of the United Kingdom post office, the U.S. Post Office carries only six times as much mail.[9] This suggests that American postmen were less productive than British postmen relative to other labor.[10] In 1974 the U.S. postman was paid 1.83 times the average income in the U.S. while the British postman received only 1.16 times the corresponding British figure.[11] This difference in relative earnings explains why, despite a similarity in organization, and despite the high proportion of temporary and substitute employees in the United States, the cost of salaries and wages (exclud-

---

[6] In the United Kingdom practically all magazines are sold in news stands or bookstores. This is because their postage is not subsidized as it is in the U.S. This might explain some of the difference in the losses. The United Kingdom reportedly also makes a profit on its telephone business while suffering a loss on its postal business. This also explains some of the difference in the losses in the U.S. and United Kingdom postal services.

[7] J. Keith Horsefield, "Some Notes on Postal Finance," *Bulletin of the Oxford Institute of Economics and Statistics*, vol. 26 (1964), reprinted in *Public Enterprise*, ed. R. Turvey (Baltimore: Penguin Books, 1968), p. 291.

[8] Ibid., p. 314.

[9] Ibid., p. 313.

[10] Yale Brozen, "The New Competition—International Markets: How Should We Adapt?" *Journal of Business of the University of Chicago*, vol. 33, no. 4 (October 1960), pp. 322, 326.

[11] See *New Society*, August 1, 1974, p. 283, for the average salary of postmen in the United Kingdom, and International Monetary Fund, *International Financial Statistics* (Washington, D.C., 1976), for average incomes in the United States and the United Kingdom.

ing pension liability) was 75 percent of total expenditures in the U.S. Postal Service compared with 64 percent in Britain.[12]

If the ratio of postal wages relative to average income in the United Kingdom is used as a standard, Postal Service employees in the United States are overpaid. This tendency agrees with the statistical computations of our model. To be more precise, if U.S. postal workers' wages were not excessive one would expect that wages of postal workers in the United States would be about double the wages of postal workers in the United Kingdom. In 1962, however, postal workers in the United States received more than three times the wages of postal workers in the United Kingdom, so it would have required a *one-third* decrease to put the wages of U.S. postal workers at a level only double that of British postal workers. This computation approximates the statistical conclusions of this study, which indicate that in 1962 postal workers were overpaid between 24 percent and 30 percent, depending on the assumed personnel costs.

The Chicago Breakdowns—1966 and 1970

The reliability of the results of this study is further corroborated by the timing of the two breakdowns of postal service in Chicago. The first breakdown occurred for three weeks in October 1966, when the thirteen-story Chicago Post Office, the world's largest postal facility (sixty acres of floor space), stopped functioning. Some believe that a six-month vacancy in the postmastership for the facility was a contributing factor to the breakdown. More striking is the fact that the breakdown occurred at a time when postal workers across the country were overpaid by only 19.4 percent, the *lowest wage differential* between actual and optimal wages for the system calculated in this study. This differential applies to the nation as a whole. In particular areas, including Chicago, the differential was a great deal lower and quite possibly negative.

The second jam-up was caused by a work stoppage that began on March 16, 1970, and ultimately involved 152,000 postal employees in 671 postal locations. The breakdown in management authority and in plant operations paralyzed service in one of the nation's biggest cities and delayed millions of cross-country letters. During this period postal workers' wages nationwide were excessive by only 20 percent on the average—the second-lowest differential calculated in this study. It is possible that in Chicago, Postal Service employees were underpaid at

---

[12] Horsefield, "Some Notes on Postal Finance," p. 290.

this time too. Under difficult working conditions the relatively low wage may well have contributed to the breakdown. The results of this study suggest that this was the case.

Factors Contributing to Excessive Wages in the Postal Service

Henry Simons held the view that a monopoly can be forced to share some of its monopoly returns with its employees.[13] If there is a relation between monopoly power and union power, then the argument could be made that unions are more prevalent and can act with more strength in monopolistic industries. The Postal Service is the only enterprise permitted to deliver letter mail. This monopoly, which involves certain controls over third-class (commercial) mail as well, is authorized by the Private Express Statutes. To police the monopoly, the postmaster general, by letter of authority filed in the department, may authorize any postal inspector or other officer of the department to search for mailable matter transported in violation of the law. To strengthen the monopoly there is a provision that private letter boxes can only be used for the reception of mail for which postage has been paid. Nor is it permissible for two or more persons or firms to reduce the amount of postage they pay by sorting, grouping, and mailing in common messages or bills.[14] In 1976 the Postal Service initiated 300 investigations into alleged violations of the antiquated Private Express Statutes, and sixty cease-and-desist orders were actually issued. These investigations and court actions restrict entry into the delivery of first-class mail and preserve the postal monopoly.

The Postal Service can and does practice monopoly pricing, but its rates are constrained by the elasticity of demand for different types of mail and by the cumbersome, legal procedures for changing rates. The evidence suggests that the demand for all types of mail service tends to be inelastic in the relevant ranges with respect to price.[15] With first-class mail the presumption is that demand is price-

---

[13] Henry Simons, "Some Reflections on Syndicalism," in *Economic Policy for a Free Society* (Chicago: University of Chicago Press, 1945), pp. 131-33, 140.

[14] U.S. Post Office Department, Office of the General Counsel, *Restrictions on Transportation of Letters—The Private Express Statutes and Interpretations*, 5th ed., July 1967, May 1972, Washington, D.C., p. 6.

[15] Baratz, *The Economics of the Postal Service*, p. 10. More recently Bernard Sobin in "Direct Testimony of Bernard Sobin on Behalf of United States Postal Service before the Postal Rate Commission: Postal Rate and Fee Increases, 1975," United States Postal Service Exh. T-43, p. 94, has calculated price and income elasticities. The price elasticities for first-class and priority mail were —0.239 and —0.23 respectively. For second-class mail they varied between —0.3 for daily

inelastic because there are only a few substitutes for the service and none similar to it.[16] Electronic communications could threaten the economic viability of the postal operations, since 70 percent of first-class mail consists of financial transactions and would be subject to this form of transmission. With respect to the Postal Service's entrance into electronic transfers Postmaster General Bailar said, "I don't see any reason why the government ought to be in a business which private industry is willing and able to take care of . . . the electronic business is a different business where we have nothing special to offer. If we jumped in, we'd be acting in a predatory manner and I don't think the government ought to do that."[17] Other classes are inelastic because rates are held artificially low. The costs of postage for most mailers are only a modest proportion of their total outlays. For private persons postage costs average 0.1 percent of per capita disposable income; for businesses 0.1 to 0.2 percent of their total operating expenditures.[18]

First-class revenues cross-subsidize other classes to the point where there appears to be no reasonable relationship between the volume of second-class mail and postal rates.[19] Notwithstanding that second-class mailers may use private delivery and that distribution costs for publishers usually constitute a significant proportion of their total costs there does not seem to be a strong relationship between their volume and rates. Third-class volume does not appear to be influenced by third-class rates except through the ratio of first-class rates.[20] Fourth-class mail competes with bus companies, the United Parcel Service, and many other companies. The United Parcel Service is the major competitor handling more than 50 percent of the parcel trade. In response to this competition the Postal Service has invested

---

newspapers and −0.1 for nonprofit and transient mail; with most being approximately −0.1. Income elasticities for different classes of mail varied from 1.0 for priority mail to .15 for transient mail, with first-class and most other types having income elasticities around 0.25.

[16] House Committee on Post Office and Civil Service, *The Impact of Postal Rate Increases*, pp. 2-3, taken from Baratz, *The Economics of the Postal Service*, p. 6. Some utility companies have been using their own employees to deliver utility bills.

[17] See Walter S. Mossberg, "Postal Service Is Losing Out on R and D," *Wall Street Journal*, May 10, 1977, p. 16.

[18] House Committee on Post Office and Civil Service, *Survey of Postal Rates*, 1960, H. Doc. 381, 86th Congress, 2nd session, p. 24, taken from Baratz, *The Economics of the Postal Service*, p. 7.

[19] Baratz, *The Economics of the Postal Service*, p. 8.

[20] Ibid., p. 10. Second-class mail constitutes 25 percent of the mail flow by weight and brings in only 2 percent of the revenue.

approximately $1 billion in regional centers for handling parcels; however, there are many cases of damaged parcels, with no increase in the quality of service. Because of routing procedures, time delays are longer. It is difficult to judge the price elasticity for fourth-class mail on the basis of existing studies but rate changes appear to have some effect on volume.[21]

The postal monopoly allows postal unions to attain excessive wages with relative ease. The postal unions, as discussed in chapter 2, are relatively strong and effective in representing their memberships and have been the active force in pushing for higher wages. H. Gregg Lewis made some estimates of the effect of unionism on wages for selected occupations and industries. He found that unions raised wages as much as 42 percent in the bituminous coal industry and 24 percent in the commercial air transportation industry. In obtaining wage agreements about 30 percent higher than efficiency criteria would require, the postal unions have successfully exploited the special characteristics of the postal industry to push their pay to the upper end of the scale.

Excessive Wages in Government Employment

While government enterprises, including the Postal Service, may not rely on the prevailing wage principle as much as the TVA, they all operate under some requirement of the sort.[22] Obviously they argue for wages comparable to the most favorable private market rates even when lower rates would clearly have attracted an adequate supply of labor. When government enterprises like the Postal Service can cite in their wage-determination process private wage rates that have been enhanced through market powers, they are building excesses into their wage structure. Queues for jobs and abnormally low voluntary quits indicate that Postal Service wages are above competitive levels.

This and other evidence indicates that employment with the Postal Service is attractive both for working conditions and for wages.[23] The pattern of excessive wages tends to be more pronounced for low-skill occupations than for high-skill occupations.[24] For instance, the mail carrier's working hours are typically shorter than the

---

[21] Ibid., pp. 10-11. The demand for fourth-class mail appears to be elastic; however, the quality of service is important to customers, and UPS appears to be much more reliable.

[22] Fogle and Lewin, "Public Sector Wage Determination," p. 2.

[23] Ibid., p. 1.

[24] Ibid., p. 15.

work week in private employment. Pay differentials between mail carriers and carriers in private employment are thus even greater when considered on an effective hourly rather than a nominal hourly basis.

Excessive wage levels for low-skill occupations are common to most government employment. Professor O. Ashenfelter concluded in his study of firemen that their union was able to raise the average hourly wage of unionized firemen by somewhere between 6 and 16 percent above the average hourly wage of nonunion firemen.[25] R. G. Ehrenberg concluded that in cities with union contracts, hourly wages for firefighters were on the average 2 to 18 percent higher.[26] Jay Chambers's study of teachers' unions found that union bargaining has increased the average salaries for teachers between 7.1 and 15.1 percent.[27]

A recent Bureau of Labor Statistics survey of eleven large urban areas found that municipal data processing, clerical, and manual workers in nine large urban areas were generally better paid than their counterparts in private industry.[28] On the basis of a survey of large private establishments, municipal salaries for the group of sixteen office clerical positions surveyed by the BLS were found to be excessive to the following degrees: New York, 1 percent; Chicago, 8 percent; Los Angeles, 18 percent; Philadelphia, 33 percent; Boston, 9 percent; New Orleans, −7 percent; Kansas City, −7 percent; Atlanta, 8 percent; Buffalo, 22 percent; Newark, 6 percent; and Houston, 21 percent. Thus only in New Orleans and Kansas City did private pay exceed municipal pay for these occupations. In the other fourteen cities the municipal wages were excessive, often substantially. Of the fifty-six cases examined, twenty-seven municipal occupations showed a wage advantage over 10 percent and nineteen had a wage advantage of at least 20 percent. These figures may be understated because the private wages used to make the comparisons were calculated only for large firms—the wages paid in small establishments typically are lower. Notwithstanding any understatement, the wage advantages found for municipal workers are compatible with the results obtained in this study for the Postal Service.

[25] O. Ashenfelter, "The Effect of Unionization on Wage in the Public Sector: The Case of Firefighters," *Industrial and Labor Relations Review*, vol. 24, no. 2 (January 1971), p. 201.

[26] R. G. Ehrenberg, "Municipal Government Structure, Unionization and the Wages of Firefighters," *Industrial and Labor Relations Review*, vol. 27, no. 1 (October 1973), p. 47.

[27] Jay Chambers, "The Impact of Teachers' Negotiations: The Empirical Results" (preliminary draft of dissertation, Berkeley, 1972), chapter 7.

[28] Fogle and Lewin, "Public Sector Wages Determination," p. 1.

Some might ask how postal unions can be successful in raising the wages of their members when the market from which the Postal Service draws most of its employees is very competitive. But the Postal Service pays higher than competitive wages. The question should be, why doesn't the postal management hire the available lower-wage workers and thereby reduce its wages to competitive levels? The answer is simply that organizational and legal rigidities (fixed wage scales, regulations, and seniority provisions) prevent any such competitive response by the postal management.[29]

Another reason why postal workers are able to raise their wages above optimal levels is their focused influence on the decision makers —members of Congress before reorganization and postal executives since. The general public hopes to keep its tax burden down, but beyond this general constraint it is usually uninformed and not especially interested in the specifics of government wage determination. The workers, on the other hand, have a strong stake in wage increases and lobby rigorously for them with little opposition. Given the customers to pay higher rates, the decision makers can readily accede to these demands. Before reorganization, unions brought strong political pressure to bear by supporting congressmen friendly to the postal workers.[30] Since the wages of some 700,000 employees were affected, the congressmen ignored the postal lobby at their own political peril. Before reorganization, then, the legislators were almost always more responsive to the postal employees than to the general public or post office customers, who suffered only slight per capita losses from overgenerous postal wages.[31]

Since the Postal Service operates on a nonprofit basis, it has no real incentives to efficiency. In this situation managers make decisions in a way to reduce their psychic rather than dollar costs. One important psychic cost is friction of employee relations in dealing with the postal unions. Employee unrest can result in breakdowns or slowdowns that would harm the postal managers' status and prestige. It is therefore "cheaper" for management to be generous with wages than to stand firmly for efficiency.

Sometimes employers—and surely the Postal Service fits the pattern—pay excessive wages simply because it is their policy to be

---

[29] See Jay Chambers, "Teachers' Unions, Collective Negotiations, and Resource Allocation in Public School Districts" (unpublished manuscript), chapter 4, pp. 1, 2, 3, 4, 17, for a discussion of the conditions affecting unions' influences on wages of teachers.

[30] Fogle and Lewin, "Public Sector Wage Determination," p. 8.

[31] Jay Chambers, "Teachers' Unions, Collective Negotiations, and Research Allocation in Public School Districts," pp. 1, 2, 3, 4, 17.

regarded as generous employers. This attitude is easily exploited by postal workers to get higher wages and their opportunities to do so have actually been enhanced by reorganization. One important reason is that postal administrators generally share the same perspective as postal workers since many of them came up through the ranks. Moreover, the compensation and status of administrators is to some extent determined by the total amount of their subordinates' salaries—an incentive *not* to economize. Thus postal managers are likely to share the benefits if postal workers are successful in negotiating higher wages.

The methods used to finance postal operations permit gross inefficiencies and the possibility for paying excessive wages. Before reorganization Congress laid down the financial principles for postal operations: private users of postal services were supposed to pay for services received while services benefiting society as a whole could be reimbursed out of the Treasury. In practice it did not work that way. There were no objective criteria for determining how large the postal subsidy should be, so it became an expedient figure. The Post Office was not then dependent upon its own resources for survival.

Since the Post Office Department was insulated from the need to worry about funds it paid minimal attention to financial controls. Its operating expenses were paid and its facilities bought from funds that had no direct connection with its receipts. The only connection between revenues and expenses was the influence that deficit financing had on the attitude of Congress during appropriation debates. The availability of supplemental appropriations provided additional security for the Post Office when costs exceeded their original appropriation. Congress generally acted rapidly in responding to the needs of the Post Office. Appropriation requests were approved in advance of many other agencies, and supplemental funds were made available on the basis of "reasonable" requests.

When the postmaster general reported a surplus—as he did in the 1880s—the legislators ordered a reduction in the rate level. This caused a disincentive to efficiency because members of the postal management felt that cost savings would be followed by reductions in the budget available to them in succeeding years. Employees received no direct benefit from productivity gains comparable to the benefits they could obtain in Congress. The lack of incentive for either postal management or employees to improve postal efficiency long ago created a climate for the granting of excessive wages to postal workers that is now ingrained.

7
POLICY CONCLUSIONS

*Postal rates have gone up again—which means that we're
getting more of a licking than the stamps do.*
Orben's Current Comedy

Regional Differentials

In small towns and rural areas postal recruitment is easy because wage
rates are above the market level. The serious turnover problem of the
Postal Service occurs in and around large cities where the labor market
is more competitive. The introduction of regional pay differentials
would seem to be a natural way to overcome this problem, but it has
met with considerable resistance from national postal unions. However, some local unions, particularly in New York and Miami, have
urged differentials for their areas.

There is precedent for regional wage differentials: some nationwide employers like the telephone system and United Parcel Service
use them. The 1967 postal reorganization bill passed by the House
provided for pay comparable with private industry on an area basis.[1]
No such provision was contained in the Senate version, however, and
none was included in the conference substitute.[2]

The postal unions base their opposition to a regional pay scale on
the increasing uniformity of wages nationally in other industries and
on the need to protect postal workers in smaller cities. The unions,
however, are coming under increasing pressure from locals in big

[1] U.S., Congress, Senate, Committee on Post Office and Civil Service, *The Postal
Reorganization Act of 1970*, July 1973 (from "Explanation of the Postal Reorganization Act and Selected Budget Materials," Washington, D.C., 1973), p. 155.
[2] Ibid.

103

cities. In 1973 locals in New York, Philadelphia, and Miami protested that they needed a wage differential to combat the high costs of urban living. Union officers may be forced to listen to them more attentively in the future.[3]

The differences in prevailing wages in different areas and cost-of-living differences are advanced as rationales for geographic differentials in wages of nationwide employers. The first proceeds from the fact that local wages for a defined occupation do in practice vary from place to place, depending on conditions of the local labor market. Because of this, each employer should set his pay levels within the range prevailing within each community, labor market area, or region in order to compete in the market. To pay less, it is said, will impede recruitment and to pay more is uneconomical and disruptive to the community wage structure.

The second rationale for area differentials proceeds on the assumption that a uniform real wage is desirable. Since the living costs vary from place to place, differentials constructed on a cost-of-living basis attempt to reach a uniform real wage level for the same job. To pay uniform real wages across the country requires the calculation of a cost-of-living index for each area or locality. Such indexes are now calculated only for major metropolitan areas. While following the same general pattern as regional wage differentials, this technique generates smaller differentials than are necessary to allow fully for the different market conditions. Moreover, in order to implement the cost-of-living differential, a base rate must be chosen by some other procedure. Assigning area differentials on the basis of prevailing wages rather than cost-of-living differences leads to wider differentials, because the factors that determine wages in labor markets are more variable than those that determine differences in the cost of living. In the first case the nationwide range is approximately 60 percent, whereas in the second the range is about 30 percent.[4] A third rationale for geographic differentials in the case of the Postal Service is that rural mail delivery is unprofitable as it is; adding excessive wages through a national uniform wage policy exacerbates the problem.

Other government blue-collar workers, though not as widespread throughout the nation as those of the Postal Service, are located both in major metropolitan areas and in sparsely populated areas. The geographical spread in wage rates for a single occupation, reflecting the range of prevailing wages in the areas involved, is wide. For light

---

[3] "Postal Unions Worry about Big City Revolt in This Week's Contract Vote," *Wall Street Journal*, July 17, 1973.

[4] Kappel Commission, *Towards Postal Excellence*, vol. 1, p. 42.

Table 20
AREA WAGE DIFFERENTIALS, NAVY DEPARTMENT
(1968)

Occupation	Pay Level (Step 3)	Differential (percent)
Laborer–light	2	76
Laborer–heavy	3	65
Helper	5	49
Auto mechanic	10	31
Electrician	11	28

Source: Kappel Commission, *Towards Postal Excellence*, vol. 1, p. 147.

laborers in the Navy Department in pay-level 2, step 3, the top hourly rate was 76 percent above the bottom rate. The percent differential for other occupations at step 3 between the highest and lowest paid locations are shown in Table 20.

The BLS study of straight-time hourly earnings in eighty-three metropolitan areas in 1965-1966 showed an interarea wage spread of nearly 100 percent for unskilled plant workers. The spread is higher for unskilled or undifferentiated labor than for skilled labor. The wage differentials of government blue-collar workers engaged in heavy labor, work similar to that of mail handlers, is 65 percent.[5] This gives some indication of the possible area differentials for mail handlers if their wages were determined on the basis of local labor market conditions.

It is possible, using the parameters of the model developed in this study, to estimate the optimal wages for different areas. The calculation of optimal wages and quits for the Postal Service depends on the quit rate and average hourly earnings for all manufacturing in the areas. With time series data the national composition of the work force and wages in all manufacturing changes little from year to year. However, when quits and wages for all manufacturing are used for Standard Metropolitan Statistical Areas (SMSAs) they do not represent the wages and quits of workers from the same industry mix. In some areas the "all manufacturing workers" category represents predominantly high-skilled workers working for high wages, in other areas predominantly unskilled workers. These differences would pose severe problems in calculating optimal wages for Postal Service workers, as would the fact that the nonpecuniary aspects of employment in

---

[5] Ibid., p. 147.

the Postal Service are not uniform across the country. For these reasons the optimal wages generated by the national model are suspect when applied to any given SMSA.

Despite these imprecisions, optimal wage and quit rates for the Postal Service were calculated in this study for different SMSAs for the year 1972 to suggest the possible range of wage differentials. With personnel costs estimated at $2,500, the optimal average hourly wages ranged from a low of $1.73 in Jackson, Mississippi, to $4.42, a range of 155 percent. The next lowest optimal wage was $2.36 in Charleston, West Virginia. Using the Charleston figure as a low point the range would be 87 percent, which is only slightly higher than the range of area differentials for similar types of work in the Navy Department. While the optimal wages calculated for any given area are not necessarily reliable for the reasons given, they do suggest that the problem of calculating area differentials is not insoluble.

Occupational Wage Differentials

It has been said that the government frequently pays more than necessary to attract low- and middle-skill workers and less than necessary to attract average-quality managers and professionals.[6] The Postal Service has little difficulty filling nonsupervisory positions, except in a few high-income areas and in a few skilled occupations like mechanics, electricians, and electronic technicians. Consequently it uses training and promotion from within its own work force to fill its technical positions.

However, the Postal Service has much less success attracting managerial and executive talent equivalent to that in private industry. The Postal Service lags behind private employers both in executive salaries and in duties and responsibilities given to managers. Nonsupervisory employees are overpaid, underproductive, and insulated. Managerial responsibility is small since the Postal Service is run by the postal manual. When this is taken into account the average salary of postmasters, supervisors, inspectors, and auditors may not be below the level for positions of comparable responsibility in industry.

Some, however, feel that the problem is not so much insufficient compensation as lack of challenge, flexibility, and opportunity for advancement on merit. Postal managers have minimal discretionary authority; on substantive matters they have to go by "the book," the *Postal Service Manual*. Innovations are unwelcome. Managers with

---

[6] Fogle and Lewin, "Public Sector Wage Determination," p. 27.

talent and imagination quickly become frustrated with rulebook operations and move on to private positions where their skills can be used to advantage.

If this view is correct, the managerial problem in the Postal Service boils down to institutional rigidity. Its solution would be decentralizing authority to give managers much more responsibility and the opportunity to win merit promotions.

Solutions to the Problem of Inefficiency in the Postal Service

In 1967 President Johnson issued Executive Order 11341 establishing the President's Commission on Postal Organization to find the causes of and solution to the inefficiency of the Post Office. After a thorough study, Chairman Frederick R. Kappel and the ten-member commission recommended the reorganization plan later adopted by Congress.

It has been over six years since reorganization took effect. Has it solved the problems? Judging from public comment no few Americans think things have gotten worse. The Postal Service today is still failing its users by not providing the quality of service they desire, failing the public by charging far more than it should, failing the taxpayers by perennially operating at a deficit, and failing its employees by stifling their potential. First-class delivery is slower than ever. Despite artifically low rates, second- and third-class are attracting private delivery competition. Postage rate increases, poor service, and increased parcel damage have caused many companies to abandon parcel post in favor of delivery by Greyhound, the airlines, United Parcel Service, and others that are cheaper and more reliable.

Plainly, the Postal Service has not been able to cut costs any more than its predecessor could. To the contrary, the postal budget has tripled in the last decade. Reorganizational changes that were to result in at least 20 percent cost reductions either have not been employed or have proved unsuccessful.

One policy that would virtually force the Postal Service to institute more efficient operations would be the repeal of the Private Express Statutes. Only the prod of competition seems likely to generate the innovations and efficiences so badly needed to modernize postal service. Competition from private carriers, even with their handicap of paying taxes, would quickly drive down first-class rates, particularly for local delivery. (In the 1840s and 1850s private express companies forced the government to lower its first-class rates from twenty-five cents to three cents—a rate that survived until 1958.) Private enterprise would run the delivery service in a more business-like manner, which could free both human and capital resources to serve the public interest. For obvious reasons this proposal is unattractive to the Postal Service and especially unattractive to the postal unions.[7]

A second solution to postal inefficiency, which does not exclude the first, would be to *denationalize* the Postal Service. There is no reason for continuing postal service as a nationalized industry merely because it has historically been a government enterprise. At the time the federal government and the Post Office were founded in 1789 there seemed little alternative to government ownership and operation of the postal system. Means of financing large-scale businesses have long since been available, however. Any need for the federal government to remain the sole supplier of postal services has vanished from memory.

As a privately run business the Postal Service would compete with other forms of communication and distribution, and would flourish or wither according to its success in meeting the needs of its customers. The public interest in the breadth, quality, and cost of services would be protected by market pressures. As private the Postal Service would pay taxes instead of being a drain on the Treasury. It would raise needed capital in the open market at a fair cost rather than wastefully through tax-financed government guarantees. In short, and unlike the present organization, it would get the job done or give way to something better.

A third, far less-ambitious proposal for dealing with the postal problem treats the principal source of inefficiency, excessive wages. The Postal Service pays far too much for labor in rural areas but with the same wage scale can attract only mediocre workers in some big cities. Regional or local wage rates are not as yet acceptable to union leaders. If the Postal Service must adhere to a uniform national wage scale, knowingly overpaying some and underpaying others, what from its viewpoint would be an optimal national wage rate?

I would suggest that this be determined by the quit rate. When the quit rate is less than 1 percent per month, any increase in postal rates to pay increased wages would be excessive and monopolistic exploitation of the public.

The coefficients of the regression equation discussed in Appendix A imply that if the annual quit rate is 12 percent, postal workers are

---

[7] See U.S. Postal Service Board of Governors, *The Private Express Statutes and Their Administration*, 1973, Washington, D.C., for what must be the most single-minded defense of the Private Express Statutes on record.

still overpaid between 16 and 20 percent.[8] The Post Office managed to live with annual quit rates of 12.39, 12.56, and 13.42 percent in the years 1967-1969. The wage excesses for those years were 21, 22, and 21 percent respectively. If the annual quit rate for postal employees were to go much above 14 percent there might be manpower problems in some areas. Under present management supervision, however, that possibility seems remote; the annual quit rates in 1973, 1974, 1975, and the first half of 1976 were 7.43, 5.64, 4.7, and 4.4 percent, respectively.

The postal rate commissioners who control rates charged for mail are usually under pressure to increase revenues by hiking postal rates to pay for wage-rate increases.[9] They should be instructed by

---

[8] The regression equation relating deviations of wages D (when personal costs are valued at $2,000) to the annual quit rate Q for the Postal Service is

$$(1) \quad D = 21.25 - .47Q \quad R^2 = .53$$
$$(5.94) \quad (-3.78)$$

where the t-values are in parentheses. Regressing in the opposite direction yields

$$Q = 37.53 - 1.19D \quad R^2 = .53$$
$$(14.11) \quad (-3.79)$$

which can be transposed into the following expression:

$$(2) \quad D = 31.53 - .84Q.$$

The coefficients of expression (1) imply that if the annual quit rate is 12 percent, postal workers are still overpaid by approximately 16 percent while expression (2) implies excessive wages of approximately 20 percent. The mean of these two estimates suggests that postal employees receive excessive wages of approximately 18 percent when the quit rate is 12 percent per year.

[9] Seymour Wenner, the chief administrative law judge for the independent Postal Rate Commission, proposed that first-class rates be cut to 8.5 cents an ounce from 10 cents and rates for other types of mail be increased from 7 percent for third-class bulk mail to 67 percent for parcel post. Mr. Wenner's decision came fourteen months after the Postal Service unilaterally raised first-class rates on a technically "temporary" basis. The rate commission and the postal governors did not approve this plan and cleared the way for the further increase in first-class mail rates to 13 cents. And even if they had approved it the Postal Service could still have filed for another rate increase, which could take effect automatically on a "temporary" basis as little as 100 days after final action is taken on the pending rate changes. But since the Postal Service cannot raise rates by more than one-third at any one time, their planned increase of first-class mail rates to 13 cents would have been frustrated.

If the commission had persisted in supporting the proposed restructuring of rates, the governors, by unanimous vote, could still have scrapped the commission's plan and imposed their own, but this process would have taken time and would have been subject to court challenge. Some postal officials think that commission support of the Wenner plan would have prompted the Postal Service to go to Congress for an additional budget subsidy, or for special legislation to allow rate boosts of more than one-third, either of which would negate the spirit of the reorganization. Wenner may yet have the last word. A trade association sued to reverse the decision (R74-1) and won in the U.S. District Court in December 1976. The basis for the court's ruling was that the United States Postal Service and Postal Rate Commission had used improper costing methods. The decision is moot because another rate case supplanted the rates in question

Congress not to grant postal rate increases if they are caused by excessive wage agreements for nonsupervisory employees, as indicated by a voluntary quit rate of less than 1 percent per month. This policy could bring some discipline to bear on Postal Service executives. When the quit rate for postal employees is around 1 percent per month, postal employees are still earning wages that on average are excessive by about 20 percent. Post offices in larger cities would be in a less advantageous position than those in more sparsely populated areas, but the strain should not be unbearable even with a uniform national pay scale. While this policy does not deal as decisively with the fundamental problems of the Postal Service as denationalization or the repeal of the Private Express Statutes, it would at least restore some equity to the relationship between postal workers and postal customers.

which has resulted in further suing. The court has all but said it will rule the same way—invalidating the current rates and perhaps restoring the 10-cent first-class stamp. (See Walter Mossberg, "Postal Service Is Told to Cut Rates on First-Class Mail, Boost Others," *Wall Street Journal*, May 29, 1975, p. 3.)

APPENDIX A

A Theoretical and Empirical Model for Evaluating Wages

Quit and Wage Rates—A Theoretical Discussion

Workers quit when job opportunities elsewhere appear to be better than their present positions. Quits are voluntary separations from employment, and as such are a supply-of-labor phenomenon. In Diagram 1 quits are represented by a shift in the supply curve from S to S'. Assuming that in the short run wages are rigid at W_0, only L_1 instead of L_0 workers would be willing to work after this shift in supply. $(L_0 - L_1)$ workers then quit.

After workers have perceived that alternative job opportunities have become more attractive, and after the supply curve has shifted from S to S', but before workers have actually quit, it would require a wage of W_1 to keep the $(L_0 - L_1)$ workers from quitting. At the existing wage, W_0, the company or companies in the industry could hire $(L_0 - L_1)$ *new* untrained workers, train them, and hold them for a while; but if the company continued to pay the same wage rate, the quits would become $(L_0 - L_1)$ workers per period of time which would yield a quit rate of $\dfrac{L_1 - L_0}{L_1 + L_0} \dfrac{1}{2} = q_0$.

To maintain employment at L_0 in the face of wage W_0, the company's net new hires would have to continue at the rate q_0 per year to replace the quits. The company could reduce its rate of quits and net new hires by raising the wage rate above W_0, say to W_0'. It would then be less difficult for the company to maintain its labor force at L_0 because the cost of net new hiring and the costs associated with processing and bringing new workers up to full productivity would decrease. If these personnel costs per new worker are P, the increase in

111

Diagram 1

THE DEMAND AND SUPPLY OF LABOR

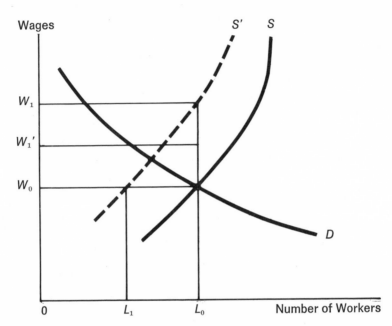

wages $\left(\dfrac{\dot{W}}{W}\right)$, would bring about a reduction in personnel costs of

$\left(\dfrac{\dot{W}}{W}\right)\sigma L_0 P$, where σ is the elasticity of the supply of labor.

On the other hand, the increase in the wage rate obviously would increase wage costs. If the wage rate is raised from W_0 to W_0', wage costs are increased by $(W_0'-W_0)L$ or $\left(\dfrac{\dot{W}}{W}\right)W_0L_0$. If a company is attempting to operate efficiently it will compare the decrease in personnel costs from new employees with the increase in wage costs to determine an optimal wage and quit rate. In this way the company can choose an optimal wage and quit rate that minimizes the total labor costs of its operations.[1] The combinations of quit and wage rates

---

[1] How would these optimal rates be chosen and what would be the condition indicating that the company had in fact chosen optimally? At a wage between W_0 and W_1 in Diagram 1 consider an increase in the wage rate $\left(\dfrac{\dot{W}}{W}\right)$. This would

from which a firm can choose can be seen in Diagram 1. For any given wage rate between W_0 and W_1, with L_0 the desired labor force, the quit rate is influenced by the shape and position of the supply curve. It is also clear from Diagram 1 that the quit and wage rates that the firm can choose are inversely related.

The Quit Rate and General Economic Conditions

The close relation between economic conditions and the quit rate is widely recognized. A worker responds to the existing economic situation in his plant or industry by quitting or not quitting. The quit rate may thus be one of the best measures of his attitude concerning the economy. In a tight labor market many job opportunities exist for workers, so the quit rate is high. Conversely, when the labor market is slack, fewer job opportunities exist elsewhere, so workers are more concerned about job security and quit less frequently. In a tight labor market employers cannot always afford to reject the poor or doubtful applicants who subsequently quit, while in a slack labor market they can be more selective.

According to time trend studies, changes in the quit rate precede changes in aggregate economic activity during periods of expansion but remain quite close to movements in aggregate economic activity during periods of contraction. In periods of expansion it is more costly for firms, in terms of their wage costs, to maintain low quit rates than in periods of contraction.[2] For instance, if a company is expanding temporarily it would be ill-advised to use increased wages to attract more workers; its wage levels would then be too high after the need

---

result in a decrease in personnel costs of $\left(\dfrac{\dot{W}}{W}\right) \sigma L_0 P$ and an increase in wage costs of $\left(\dfrac{\dot{W}}{W}\right)$. $W L_0$. The efficient firm would choose that wage level which minimizes the sum of its wage and personnel costs. As the wage rate is increased from W_0 towards W_1 it will reach the wage rate W_1' where the decrease in personnel costs is just equal to the increase in wage costs. The equilibrium condition is

$$\left(\frac{\dot{W}}{W}\right) \sigma L P = \left(\frac{\dot{W}}{W}\right) W L_0$$

or $\quad \sigma P = W.$

Given the elasticity of the supply of labor and the average personnel costs per new recruit, the optimum wage rate can be calculated from the above expression.

[2] Herbert S. Parnes, "The Labor Force and Labor Market," *Employment Relations Research* (New York: Harper and Brothers, 1960), p. 36.

for extra workers ceased. If an industry were contracting, there would be no need to replace all separations, so retraining costs could be avoided. In general, then, it is inadvisable for businesses to try to fight cyclical movements in quit rates with a wage policy. A wage policy for a firm or an industry should be keyed to an average quit rate free of business cycle fluctuations. Since the quit rates for all industries are closely related to the business cycle, the influence of the business cycle on the quit rates for the individual industries should be removed. The quit rate for all manufacturing scores high as an indicator of economic activity (71 out of 100 on the scale adopted by Geoffrey H. Moore and Julius Shiskin).[3] This study removes the influence of the level of economic activity on the postal quit rate, in order to measure the effect of postal wage rates on quit rates, by using the quit rate for all manufacturing, Q_m.

Empirical Measures of the Postal Wage and Quit Rates

The average hourly wages variable measures the earnings of only the production workers in an industry, while the quit rate pertains to all employees in an industry. While the two groups do not coincide exactly, the discrepancy is not serious. The Postal Service calculates its quit rate for all employees, both supervisory and nonsupervisory. It would have been better for our purposes had the quit rate been available for the nonsupervisory employees only. However, in the case of the Postal Service, the inclusion of the supervisory employees for purpose of calculating the quit rate is even less serious than in manufacturing, since supervisors are greatly outnumbered by nonsupervisory employees. Casual knowledge indicates that the quit rate among the supervisors is higher than the quit rate among nonsupervisors, so inclusion of the supervisors tends to increase the quit rate slightly.

The annual quit rates for the Postal Service are calculated by dividing the total number of quits for the year by the average employment over the year, including temporary Christmas help. For the calculation of average employment and the quit rate, figures from Alaska have been used since January 1959, and figures from Hawaii have been used since August 1959. Figures for 1970, 1971, and 1972 exclude employees in the Nonceiling Youth Program and public service

---

[3] Paul A. Armknecht and John F. Early, "Quits in Manufacturing—A Study of Their Causes," *Monthly Labor Review*, November 1972, p. 31.

career employees. The series of quit rates and wage rates for the Postal Service begins in 1958. Figures are unavailable for previous years. Since postal quit rates for 1965 and 1966 were unavailable the regressions for the Post Office and Postal Service do not use observations for these years.

Postal wages for the fiscal years 1958 to 1971 were calculated from "Changes in Pay Distribution for Postal Field Service Employees," obtained from the Postal Service. This source contains a distribution of employees by salary categories in increments of $500 and contains a mean salary for all postal field service employees as of June 30 in each of the years from 1958 through 1971. The average hourly wage for the regular Postal Service employees was calculated by dividing the mean annual salary by 2,016, the average number of hours worked; for 1971, the divisor was 2,008. The average wage of Postal Service employees for 1972 was calculated from figures contained in the appendix to the *Budget of the United States for Fiscal Year 1974*. The table is titled "Postal Service—Consolidated Schedule of Permanent Positions Paid from Funds Available to the U.S. Postal Service." The rates used are the Postal Service schedule grades PS-1 to PS-12. To check the comparability of the average hourly wages calculated this way with the average hour wages calculated using the distribution of employees by salary range for increments of $500, the wage was calculated using the data from the *Budget of the United States* for the years 1970, 1971, and 1972, although the figures calculated this way were used only for 1972. The wage calculated in 1970 and 1971 using the budget data was slightly higher in 1970 (by $0.13); slightly lower in 1971 (by $0.10). This check suggested that the wage calculated using the budget data for 1972 would be substantially accurate.

The Empirical Relationship between the Wage and Quit Rates

Several studies have examined how the wage and quit rates vary among manufacturing industries but do not compare the relationship between the wage and quit rates within a given industry. In some industries the quit rate might respond to wage levels; in others institutional forces might predominate to the point where measured wage effects are imperceptible; some industries might fall between these two extremes. Even when there are no wage incentives for workers to leave their firms, there is a normal level of voluntary turnover for any number of personal reasons. There are so many variables other than wages that affect the labor market that it is impossible to isolate their independent influence on the quit rate when they are all used in the same model. In the model constructed in this study the factors that influence the quit rate, other than the wage rate and general economic conditions, are reflected in the value of the constant term. The variations in the quit rates that result from a comparison of the wage rate in a particular industry W_i with the wage level obtainable elsewhere are represented in the model by the ratio of the industry i wage to the all manufacturing wage level $\left(\dfrac{W_i}{W_m}\right)$. The business cycle fluctuations in a quit rate for an industry, i, Q_i, are removed by including the quit rate for all manufacturing, Q_m, in the regression equation. The empirical relationship estimated for industry i is then

$$Q_i = aQ_m{}^b \left(\frac{W_i}{W_m}\right)^c . \tag{1}$$

In natural log form this becomes

$$\ln Q_i = \ln a + b \ln Q_m + c(\ln W_i - \ln W_m). \tag{2}$$

In equation (2) $\ln a$ is the natural log of the quit rate that would exist in industry i if the annual quit rate for all manufacturing were 1 percent per year and there were no wage differential between all manufacturing and industry i. Except for the effects of general business conditions and the wage differential on quits, all other influences are reflected in the value $\ln a$. The parameter a captures all the non-wage, nonbusiness-cycle conditions of employment influencing the quit rate and can be thought of as the annual quit rate for industry i that would be attributable solely to the nonpecuniary aspects of employment in the industry relative to all other industries.

The parameter b in equation (2) is an elasticity of response in the quit rate of industry i to the business fluctuations reflected in changes in the quit rate for all manufacturing. A value of b approximating 1 indicates that for a 1 percent increase in Q_m (the quit rate for all manufacturing), Q_i (the quit rate for industry i) increases by 1 percent. The parameter c is an elasticity of response in the quit rate in industry i to changes in the relative wage ratio $\left(\dfrac{W_i}{W_m}\right)$. A negative sign for c indicates that as wages in industry i rise relative to the wages for all manufacturing, quits in industry i decrease. The value of c indicates the percentage by which Q_i would diminish in response to a 1 percent increase in $\left(\dfrac{W_i}{W_m}\right)$.

The parameters ln a, b, and c of equation (2) were estimated econometrically for twenty-one two-digit industries where data were available and for the Postal Service. These are listed in columns 1, 2, and 3 of Table A-1. Annual data for these industries covered the years 1958-1972. A partial first difference estimating technique was used to try to eliminate some of the serial correlation in the residuals. The Durban-Watson statistics and the ρ-values of the differential factors are listed in column 5 of Table A-1. The R^2s in column 4, which indicate the percentage of the variation in the quit rates which can be accounted for by the variables used to explain them, are calculated from the untransformed residuals and are adjusted for degrees of freedom. Columns 4 and 5 refer to regression equations described in columns 1-3 and columns 6-8. All of the R^2s are in excess of 0.72, indicating that most of the variation in industry quit rates is "explained" by the business fluctuations and wage-rate changes. Other employment factors, accounted for in the constant terms, have been fairly stable. From Table A-1, column 1, it can be seen that for the twenty-two industries considered, all the estimates of the constant terms, except for two, are significant at the 10 percent level while twelve are significant at the 5 percent level. In column 2, it can be seen that all the estimates of b are significant at the 5 percent level or better. In all but two of the industries, namely Food and kindred products and Printing and publishing, the value of the estimate of c was negative as expected, although the t-values indicating the degree of confidence one can place in the estimates of the coefficients are not impressive. However, the t-value for the Postal Service, our main concern in this study, is -2.872, which is significant at the .01 level using a one-tailed test. In layman's language this means that knowing in advance that the sign of the coefficient should be negative, we can be 99 percent sure that our estimate is not zero. *The t-values for all the coefficients for the Postal Service are significant at the 1 percent level or better.*

Because of the regression bias the values of the coefficients in column 3 are low absolute estimates for the parameter c. When they are used in the optimal wage model, they generate lower estimates of optimal wages. To calculate upper absolute estimates of the parameter c in equation (2), I reversed the relative wage and industry quit terms and produced the equation printed over columns 6-9 of Table A-1 which contains α, β, and γ.[4] To transform the coefficients of this equa-

---

[4] I am grateful to Milton Friedman for suggesting in private correspondence this alternative way of estimating the parameters. The underlying statistical theory is in K. A. Brownlee, *Statistical Theory and Methodology in Science and Engineering*, 2nd ed. (New York: John Wiley and Sons, 1965), pp. 404-10.

Table A-1

QUITS AND WAGES

Industry (SIC #)	$\ln Q_i = \ln a + b \ln Q_m + c(\ln W_i - \ln W_m)$					$\ln W_i - \ln W_m = \ln \alpha + \beta \ln Q_m + \gamma \ln Q_i$		
	$\ln a$ (t-value) (1)	b (t-value) (2)	c (t-value) (3)	R^2 (standard error) (4)	D-W (ρ) (5)	$\ln \alpha$ (t-value) (6)	β (t-value) (7)	γ (t-value) (8)
Postal Service	−2.080** (−3.378)	1.491** (6.590)	−2.706** (−2.872)	.796 (.169)	1.785 (0)	−.509** (−3.075)	.337** (4.076)	−.177** (−2.872)
Ordnance & accessories 19	−1.448* (−1.362)	1.279** (5.164)	−4.190* (−1.341)	.722 (.150)	2.005 (.9)	.081 (.812)	.032 (.809)	−.034* (−1.341)
Lumber & wood products 24	.406** (1.820)	1.013** (16.794)	−.700* (−1.699)	.962 (.053)	1.541 (0)	−.170 (1.082)	.355** (2.072)	−.297* (−1.699)
Furniture & fixtures 25	−.937** (−2.204)	1.360** (15.115)	−1.390 (−1.186)	.954 (.080)	.791 (0)	−.388** (−4.839)	.142* (1.546)	−.081 (−1.186)
Stone, clay, & glass products 32		1.090** (15.748)	−.337 (−.365)	.984 (.047)	1.056 (1.0)		.025 (.255)	−.033 (−.365)
Primary metal industries 33	−1.865** (−3.185)	1.534** (13.110)	−1.735 (1.080)	.943 (.108)	1.448 (0)	.166 (1.236)	.058 (.711)	−.055 (1.080)
Fabricated metal products 34	−.964** (−6.407)	1.341** (26.271)	−1.550* (−1.587)	.983 (.048)	1.145 (0)	−.102 (−1.170)	.175** (1.743)	−.120* (−1.587)
Machinery, except electrical 35	−.155 (−.767)	1.175** (14.072)	−5.687** (−3.815)	.949 (.064)	1.319 (0)	−.005 (−.188)	.133** (4.952)	−.100** (−3.815)
Electrical equipment & supplies 36	.513 (1.646)	.786** (7.820)	−2.341 (−1.168)	.838 (.098)	1.354 (0)	.055 (1.172)	.028 (.781)	−0.47 (−1.168)
Transportation equipment 37	−.441** (2.982)	1.171** (19.816)	−2.188** (−3.506)	.975 (.047)	1.829 (0)	−.088* (−1.461)	.309** (4.201)	−.241** (−3.506)

Industry							
Instruments & related products 38	.449** (2.350)	.778** (12.592)	−.979 (−.637)	.923 (.062)	1.383 (0)	.026 (.578)	.031 (.680)	−.036 (−.637)
Miscellaneous manufacturing industries 39		.998** (11.327)	−1.285 (−1.138)	.950 (.060)	1.436 (1.0)		.073 (1.040)	−.076 (−1.138)
Food & kindred products 20	.936** (3.478)	.822** (9.942)	.952 (.893)	.973 (.049)	2.318 (.7)	−.092 (−.895)	−.062 (−.908)	.071 (.893)
Tobacco manufactures 21	1.184* (1.558)	.549** (2.803)	−1.187 (−.906)	.884 (.120)	1.418 (.9)	.053 (.286)	.021 (.370)	−.059 (−.906)
Textile mill products 22	1.486** (3.586)	.726** (9.749)	−.535 (−.710)	.987 (.042)	1.310 (.9)	−.279 (1.251)	.097 (1.129)	−.082 (−.710)
Apparel & other textile products 23		.702** (9.167)	−1.850** (−3.171)	.909 (.052)	1.845 (1.0)		.170** (2.733)	−.246** (−3.171)
Paper & allied products 26	−.938** (−3.418)	1.275** (13.650)	−1.189 (−1.334)	.953 (.074)	1.270 (0)	−.256** (−2.657)	.205** (1.899)	−.117 (−1.334)
Printing & publishing 27		.677** (8.095)	.574 (.750)	.918 (.054)	1.750 (1.0)		−.021 (−.266)	.078 (.750)
Chemicals & allied products 28	−.379* (−1.463)	.992** (11.290)	−1.735 (−1.167)	.913 (.081)	.952 (0)	.012 (.230)	.083* (1.529)	−.064 (−1.167)
Petroleum & coal products 29	.498 (.430)	.651** (3.005)	−.444 (−.166)	.829 (.133)	1.229 (.9)	.299** (3.132)	.001 (.023)	−.006 (−.166)
Rubber & plastics products 30	−.937** (−3.539)	1.339** (15.801)	−1.711* (−1.423)	.974 (.065)	1.057 (0)	.036 (.408)	.083 (.909)	−.091* (−1.423)
Leather & leather products 31	.962** (2.531)	.848** (10.184)	−.713 (−.955)	.964 (.051)	2.430 (.9)	−.145 (.804)	.082 (.807)	−.107 (−.955)

** Indicates significant at 5 percent level.
* Indicates significant at 10 percent level.

tion into estimates of the parameters in equation (2), I used the new estimates $\bar{a}, \bar{b},$ and $\bar{c}$ where

$$\ln\bar{a} = \frac{\ln\alpha}{\gamma}, \bar{b} = -\frac{\beta}{\gamma} \text{ and } \bar{c} = \frac{1}{\gamma}.$$

The values of $\bar{a}, \bar{b},$ and $\bar{c}$ for the nineteen industries are listed in Table A-2. In this table the two industries, Food and kindred products and Printing and publishing, are dropped because they have positive c-values. The Petroleum and coal products industry is also dropped because of the extremely low t-value of the coefficient. While both sets of estimates a, b, c and $\bar{a}, \bar{b},$ and $\bar{c}$ could be used to calculate the optimal wage, $a, b,$ and c yield minimum values for the optimal wage.[5] Only $\bar{a}, \bar{b},$ and $\bar{c}$ are used in the calculations of this study.

The values of $\bar{a}$ for different industries in Table A-2 indicate the influence of nonwage employment conditions on quits in their respective industries. If the value of $\bar{a}$ is low, as it is for the Postal Service, Fabricated metal products, Furniture and fixtures, or Textile mill products, this indicates that fewer of the quits are attributable to nonwage conditions of employment in the industry. Nonwage conditions of employment in industries such as Ordnance and accessories contribute more to quits. The quit rate for an industry having a value of 1 for the parameter $\bar{b}$ responds to business conditions in the same way as the quit rate for All manufacturing. If $\bar{b}$ is greater than 1 as it is for the Postal Service the quit rate for this industry fluctuates more in percentage terms over the business cycle than the quit rate for All manufacturing. If $\bar{b}$ is less than 1, as it is for Tobacco and tobacco products or Electrical machinery, this indicates that the quit rate fluctuates less in percentage terms over the business cycle than the quit rate for All manufacturing.

The values of $\bar{c}$ indicate how sensitive the quit rate in an industry is to changes in wage differentials between that industry and All manufacturing. Industries such as Ordnance and accessories which have $\bar{c}$-values around -30 indicate that the decision of workers to quit is extremely sensitive to wage differentials between their industry and others. Workers in industries such as Lumber and wood products, Apparel and other textile products, Transportation equipment or the Postal Service, with $\bar{c}$-values between -3.4 and -5.6, are less sensitive to wage differentials between their industry and others in their quit decisions. The fact that quit rates are not sensitive to the wage

---

[5] I have used both sets of parameters to calculate an optimal wage with the model described in this appendix. The parameters $a, b,$ and c do in fact yield minimum values for the optimal wage and $a, b,$ and $c,$ maximum values.

Table A-2

$$\ln Q_i = \ln \bar{a} + \bar{b}\ln Q_m + \bar{c}(\ln W_i - \ln W_m)$$

MAXIMUM ESTIMATES OF PARAMETERS

Industry[a]	In a	a	b	c
Postal Service	−2.8757	.05638	1.9040	− 5.6497
Machinery, except electrical	−0.0500	.95123	1.3300	−10.000
Transportation equipment	− .3651	.69413	1.2822	− 4.1494
Apparel & other textile products	0.0	1.000	.6911	− 4.0650
Ordnance & accessories	2.3824	10.83087	.9412	−29.4118
Lumber & wood products	− .5724	.56417	1.1953	− 3.3670
Fabricated metal products	−8.3417	.00024	1.4583	− 8.3333
Paper and paper products	−2.1880	.11214	1.7521	− 8.5470
Rubber & plastics	.3956	1.48527	.9121	−10.9890
Furniture & fixtures	−4.7901	.0083	1.7531	−12.3457
Stone, clay, & glass products	0.0	1.000	.7576	−30.3030
Primary metal products	3.0182	20.45444	1.0545	−18.1818
Electrical machinery	1.1702	3.22263	.5957	−21.2766
Instruments & related products	.7222	2.05896	.8611	−27.7778
Miscellaneous manufacturing industries	0.0	1.000	.9605	−13.1579
Tobacco & tobacco products	.8983	2.45542	.3559	−16.9491
Textile mill products	−3.4024	.03329	1.1829	−12.1951
Chemicals & allied products	.1875	1.2062	1.2969	−15.6250
Leather & leather products	−1.3551	.87327	.7664	− 9.3458

[a] The industries are arranged according to the level of significance of the estimate for c in column 3 of Table A-1. All industries in the top section have estimates of c which are significant at the 5 percent level or better. Those in the middle section have estimates of c which are significant at the 10 percent level or better.

differentials between the employing industry and others in some cases does not necessarily mean that the quit rate is not influenced by relative wage rates. Quit rates may be high with substantial movement caused by wage differentials within an industry, notwithstanding a lack of correlation between the quit rate and wage differentials with other industries. The following parameters were estimated for the Postal Service:

$$\ln\bar{a} = -2.88 \qquad \bar{a} = .056$$
$$\bar{b} = 1.90 \qquad \bar{c} = -5.65$$

The parameter $\bar{a}$ captures all the nonwage, nonbusiness-cycle conditions of employment influencing the quit rate and is that part of the annual quit rate in the Postal Service attributable solely to the nonpecuniary aspects of employment in the Postal Service relative to other industries. The low value of $\bar{a}$, .056, indicates that the nonpecuniary aspects of employment in the Postal Service relative to other industries are responsible for very few quits, on average, less than 1 percent per year.

The parameter $\bar{b}$ is an elasticity of response in the postal quit rate to the business fluctuations that are reflected in the quit rate for All manufacturing. A value of $\bar{b}$ of 1.90 indicates that for a 10 percent increase in the annual quit rate for All manufacturing, say from 22 to 24.2 percent, the quit rate in the Postal Service would increase almost 20 percent, say from 8 to 9.6 percent. The value 1.90 of parameter $\bar{b}$ is the highest for all industries examined, which suggests that in percentage terms the annual quit rate of the Postal Service fluctuates more over the business cycle than the quit rate of any other two-digit industry. However, since the average annual quit rate of the Postal Service is smaller than for any two-digit industry, the absolute changes in the Postal Service quit rate over the cycle are not large.

The parameter $\bar{c}$ indicates how sensitive the quit rate in the Postal Service is to changes in wage rates. It is an elasticity of response in the postal quit rate to changes in the wage differential between the Postal Service and All manufacturing. The value of -5.65 for $\bar{c}$ indicates that if postal wages rise 10 percent relative to wages for All manufacturing the annual quit rate for the Postal Service would fall 56 percent from about 8 to 3.5 percent per year. On the other hand if Postal Service wages were excessive by 30 percent, and if this resulted in the abnormally low quit rate of 8 percent, a decrease in postal wages of 10 percent relative to the wages in All manufacturing would result in a quit rate of approximately 12 rather than 8 percent per year even though postal wages would remain excessive by 20 percent. If it were desirable to reduce postal wages by a further 10 percent relative to the wages for All manufacturing, this would result in an annual Postal Service quit rate of approximately 18 percent while leaving postal wages excessive by 10 percent. If postal wages were reduced by still another 10 percent, to parity with the wages of All manufacturing, the annual quit rate for the Postal Service would jump to around 27 percent. In these hypothetical examples the trade-off between the quit rate and wage rate for the Postal Service is determined by the value of the parameter $\bar{c}$.

The Determination of an Expression for Optimal Wages

The total labor costs of a firm can be divided into two parts: (1) personnel costs and (2) wage costs. Personnel costs are associated with advertising, interviewing, and hiring new recruits, bringing them up to full productivity, and the eventual termination costs associated with separating them. The average personnel costs associated with hiring a new recruit are P dollars. If the quit rate for a firm in industry i is Q_i per hundred employees per year and the firm desires to maintain a labor force for L_0 workers, the annual personnel costs of maintaining its labor force is $\left(\dfrac{Q_i}{100}\right) \cdot P \cdot L_0$.[6]

Now if we assume that the average hourly wage paid by a firm in industry i is W_i, and that each employee works 2,000 hours per year, the wage costs associated with a labor force of L_0 is $W_i(2000)L_0$. The total labor costs per year (TLC) is then the addition of the personnel costs and the wage costs, namely,

$$TLC = \left(\frac{Q_i}{100}\right) \cdot P \cdot L_0 + W_i(2000)L_0. \tag{3}$$

Now substituting from expression (1) into expression (3) for Q_i yields

$$TLC = \left(\frac{aQ_m{}^b}{100W_m{}^c}\right)W_i{}^c \cdot P \cdot L_0 + W_i(2000)L_0. \tag{4}$$

As W_i, the wage rate in industry i, is increased, personnel costs diminish (since $c < 0$) because of a decreased quit rate, but wage costs increase. If W_i is decreased, personnel costs increase but wage costs decrease. The firm that desires to operate efficiently will pay a wage that minimizes TLC; this wage is considered to be the optimal wage.

---

[6] The assumption that firms desire to maintain the size of their work force might be questioned. If so replacement costs should refer not to quits but to those who are replaced. New hires would then be used in this expression instead of quits. As a matter of fact, monthly quits and new hires for ninety-nine four-digit SIC manufacturing industries are closely correlated (the correlation coefficient between them is 0.91); for the period 1958-1963, as are other accessions (rehires) and layoffs (the correlation coefficient between these two variables is 0.95). Thus workers who quit are likely to be replaced, and those who are laid off are likely to be rehired. See Lester G. Telser, *Competition, Collusion and Game Theory* (Chicago and New York: Aldine Atherton, 1972), p. 340.

To find the optimal wage, W^*, let $\dfrac{dTLC}{dW_i} = 0$ and solve for W_i.[7]

$$\frac{dTLC}{dW_i} = ca\, \frac{Q_m{}^b\, W_i{}^{c-1}}{100 W_m{}^c} \cdot P \cdot L_0 + 2000\, L_0 = 0$$

Therefore

$$\frac{ca\, Q_m{}^b\, W_i{}^{c-1}}{100 W_m{}^c} P = -2000$$

and

$$W_i{}^* = \left[\frac{-2000(100) W_m{}^c}{ca Q_m{}^b\, P} \right]^{\frac{1}{c-1}} \qquad \text{where } a,b>0 \qquad (5)$$
$$c<0.$$

The quit rate associated with $W_i{}^*$ is the optimal rate and is found by substituting $W_i{}^*$ into (1) for W_i. The optimal quit rate $Q_i{}^*$ is then

$$Q_i{}^* = a Q_m{}^b\, W_m{}^{\frac{c}{c-1}} \left[\frac{-2000(100)}{ca\, Q_m{}^b\, P} \right]^{\frac{c}{c-1}}. \qquad (6)$$

It might be noted that in the derivation of the optimal wage and quit rates, the size of the labor force does not affect the optimal values.

In a more general model, personnel costs, the quit rate, the new hires rate, the layoff rate, the rehire rate, and the wage rate would all be interrelated endogenous variables and would be determined simultaneously. The model would then describe the long-run equilibrium

---

[7] The objection might be raised that if the average quality of postal workers could be increased through the payment of higher wages, fewer workers would be needed. Since this possibility is not considered in the model, the optimal wage as determined in this study might be understated. However, union rules of various kinds restrain employers from taking full advantage of higher relative wages to raise the average quality of the working force. Though higher real wages may attract a better quality of worker, he may not work at his full capability as a result of uniform work rules or poor supervision. This certainly seems to the case in the Postal Service, which operates strictly by the book and actually treats as infractions any deviations that might enhance productivity. Thus even if better-quality workers are hired at higher real wages it does not follow that productivity will necessarily be higher. The Kappel Commission calculated, on the basis of real Post Office wages in the forty-three metropolitan areas, the effect of salary discrepancies on productivity. Productivity was measured by the number of first-handling pieces per total clerk/mail handler hour (see *Towards Postal Excellence*, vol. 1, p. 132). The correlation coefficient between the salary discrepancies in percentage terms and productivity as described above is 0.19. This seems to indicate that in the Postal Service the real wage level has little direct impact on productivity (see *Towards Postal Excellence*, vol. 4, p. 5.51, 5.201). The influence of the wage level on productivity could not be measured for other industries because detailed data on productivity of labor were not available.

Table A-3

CURRENT DOLLAR PERSONNEL COSTS THAT WOULD MAKE ACTUAL WAGES OPTIMAL
(dollars)

Year	Postal Service	Ordnance and Accessories	Lumber and Wood Products	Furniture and Fixtures	Stone, Clay, and Glass Products
58	22311	22923	4958	2487	2286
59	10299	11753	3654	1320	1214
60	11639	13540	4085	1648	2452
61	20898	20838	4718	1696	2655
62	12844	17984	3879	1182	2415
63	19093	22121	3923	1160	2174
64	16790	25204	3808	1011	1869
65	12802	21679	2922	712	1817
66	7046	7051	2047	430	1324
67	8218	2713	2602	661	1353
68	9079	3191	3163	1003	4671
69	8258	2359	3145	948	5883
70	18637	2616	4857	1469	8389
71	37657	3678	6177	1695	15413
72	27446	3353	5011	1174	17390

Year	Primary Metal Products	Fabricated Metal Products	Machinery, except Electrical	Electrical Machinery	Transportation Equipment
58	5495	5010	5149	1470	13103
59	5064	3507	3870	1263	9784

Table A-3 (continued)

Year	Primary Metal Products	Fabricated Metal Products	Machinery, except Electrical	Electrical Machinery	Transportation Equipment
60	4375	4544	4642	1561	12493
61	5413	5154	5352	1839	13882
62	4516	4013	4696	1424	12280
63	3916	3920	4658	1336	12964
64	3384	3592	4557	1105	12090
65	2295	2583	3423	913	9548
66	1409	1724	2395	571	6500
67	1104	2037	2692	709	7628
68	2369	2695	3580	1624	9148
69	2701	2505	3659	1497	8574
70	2353	3661	4933	1816	11478
71	3820	4772	6209	2364	17293
72	6742	3976	5543	1710	14482

Year	Instruments and Related Products	Miscellaneous Manufacturing Industries	Tobacco and Tobacco Products	Textile Mill Products	Apparel and Other Textile Products
58	1373	262	25	498	3541
59	1217	176	20	401	2622
60	1392	195	24	491	2805
61	1701	185	37	462	3118
62	1335	168	42	399	2892
63	1073	163	46	554	2895

Year	Paper and Paper Products	Chemicals and Allied Products	Rubber and Plastics	Leather and Leather Products
58	4577	3075	3839	1065
59	2763	2508	2955	722
60	3828	3641	3094	827
61	4908	4528	3389	884
62	3700	3636	2863	758
63	3954	3573	2413	735
64	3732	3412	2328	758
65	2629	2612	1846	661
66	1518	1606	1157	489
67	2017	1848	1141	726
68	2682	2913	1871	1250
69	2556	3037	1693	1239
70	4196	3625	1802	1487
71	6273	6479	2301	1437
72	5104	5725	1914	1131

Year					
64	822	149	424	40	2927
65	689	118	390	76	2450
66	546	85	303	78	1964
67	696	127	416	79	2613
68	1437	225	771	281	3532
69	1350	236	743	277	3319
70	1839	310	878	763	3670
71	1794	325	954	1139	3939
72	1315	247	810	1792	3420

Table A-4
OPTIMAL HOURLY WAGES

Industry	Year	Actual Wage	Estimated Personnel Costs per Recruit					
			$500	$1000	$1500	$2000	$2500	$3000
Postal Service	58	2.39	1.30	1.44	1.53	1.60	1.66	1.70
	59	2.40	1.47	1.63	1.73	1.81	1.87	1.92
	60	2.41	1.45	1.61	1.71	1.78	1.84	1.89
	61	2.63	1.44	1.60	1.70	1.78	1.84	1.89
	62	2.62	1.55	1.72	1.83	1.91	1.97	2.03
	63	2.85	1.59	1.76	1.87	1.96	2.02	2.08
	64	2.92	1.66	1.84	1.96	2.04	2.11	2.17
	65	3.08	1.83	2.03	2.16	2.25	2.33	2.39
	66	3.19	2.08	2.31	2.46	2.57	2.65	2.73
	67	3.26	2.08	2.31	2.45	2.56	2.65	2.72
	68	3.44	2.17	2.41	2.56	2.67	2.77	2.84
	69	3.64	2.34	2.60	2.76	2.89	2.99	3.07
	70	4.03	2.31	2.56	2.72	2.84	2.94	3.02
	71	4.51	2.33	2.59	2.75	2.88	2.97	3.06
	72	4.79	2.62	2.91	3.09	3.23	3.34	3.43
Machinery, except electrical	58	2.37	1.87	1.99	2.07	2.12	2.17	2.20
	59	2.48	2.01	2.14	2.22	2.28	2.33	2.37
	60	2.55	2.03	2.17	2.25	2.31	2.36	2.40
	61	2.62	2.06	2.20	2.28	2.34	2.39	2.43
	62	2.71	2.16	2.30	2.39	2.45	2.50	2.54
	63	2.78	2.22	2.36	2.45	2.52	2.57	2.61

64	2.70	2.66	2.60	2.54	2.44	2.29	2.87
65	2.86	2.82	2.76	2.69	2.59	2.43	2.96
66	3.10	3.05	2.99	2.91	2.80	2.63	3.09
67	3.17	3.11	3.05	2.97	2.86	2.69	3.19
68	3.26	3.20	3.14	3.06	2.95	2.77	3.36
69	3.48	3.42	3.35	3.26	3.14	2.95	3.58
70	3.57	3.51	3.44	3.36	3.23	3.04	3.77
71	3.71	3.65	3.58	3.49	3.36	3.16	3.99
72	4.03	3.97	3.89	3.79	3.65	3.43	4.27

Transportation equipment

58	1.80	1.73	1.66	1.57	1.45	1.27	2.51
59	2.00	1.93	1.85	1.75	1.62	1.41	2.64
60	1.98	1.91	1.83	1.73	1.60	1.40	2.74
61	1.98	1.91	1.83	1.73	1.60	1.40	2.80
62	2.11	2.04	1.95	1.85	1.71	1.49	2.91
63	2.16	2.09	2.00	1.89	1.74	1.52	3.01
64	2.25	2.17	2.08	1.97	1.82	1.59	3.09
65	2.46	2.37	2.27	2.15	1.98	1.73	3.21
66	2.76	2.67	2.55	2.42	2.23	1.95	3.33
67	2.77	2.67	2.56	2.42	2.24	1.95	3.44
68	2.88	2.78	2.66	2.52	2.33	2.03	3.69
69	3.10	2.99	2.86	2.71	2.50	2.19	3.89
70	3.08	2.97	2.84	2.69	2.49	2.17	4.06
71	3.13	3.02	2.89	2.73	2.53	2.21	4.44
72	3.48	3.36	3.22	3.04	2.81	2.46	4.73

Apparel and other textile products

58	1.42	1.37	1.31	1.24	1.14	0.99	1.54
59	1.53	1.47	1.41	1.33	1.23	1.07	1.56
60	1.54	1.48	1.42	1.34	1.24	1.08	1.59
61	1.55	1.49	1.43	1.35	1.25	1.09	1.64
62	1.62	1.56	1.50	1.41	1.31	1.14	1.69

Table A-4 (continued)

Industry	Year	Actual Wage	Estimated Personnel Costs per Recruit					
			$500	$1000	$1500	$2000	$2500	$3000
	63	1.73	1.16	1.33	1.45	1.53	1.60	1.66
	64	1.79	1.20	1.38	1.49	1.58	1.65	1.71
	65	1.83	1.28	1.47	1.59	1.68	1.76	1.82
	66	1.89	1.39	1.59	1.73	1.83	1.91	1.98
	67	2.03	1.41	1.62	1.75	1.86	1.94	2.01
	68	2.21	1.45	1.67	1.81	1.91	2.00	2.07
	69	2.31	1.55	1.78	1.93	2.04	2.13	2.21
	70	2.39	1.58	1.82	1.97	2.08	2.18	2.26
	71	2.49	1.64	1.88	2.03	2.15	2.25	2.33
	72	2.61	1.78	2.04	2.21	2.34	2.45	2.54
Ordnance and accessories	58	2.51	2.19	2.24	2.27	2.29	2.31	2.32
	59	2.57	2.29	2.35	2.38	2.40	2.42	2.43
	60	2.65	2.35	2.41	2.44	2.47	2.48	2.50
	61	2.75	2.41	2.46	2.50	2.52	2.54	2.56
	62	2.83	2.49	2.55	2.58	2.61	2.63	2.64
	63	2.93	2.56	2.62	2.66	2.68	2.70	2.72
	64	3.03	2.64	2.70	2.74	2.76	2.78	2.80
	65	3.13	2.74	2.80	2.84	2.87	2.89	2.91
	66	3.17	2.88	2.95	2.99	3.02	3.04	3.06
	67	3.18	2.99	3.05	3.10	3.13	3.15	3.17
	68	3.26	3.05	3.12	3.16	3.19	3.21	3.23
	69	3.42	3.23	3.31	3.35	3.38	3.41	3.43
	70	3.61	3.41	3.48	3.53	3.56	3.59	3.61

	Year							
	71	3.85	3.60	3.68	3.73	3.76	3.79	3.81
	72	4.09	3.84	3.93	3.98	4.02	4.05	4.07
Lumber and wood products	58	1.79	1.00	1.17	1.29	1.37	1.45	1.51
	59	1.87	1.12	1.31	1.44	1.54	1.62	1.69
	60	1.89	1.10	1.29	1.42	1.52	1.60	1.67
	61	1.95	1.10	1.29	1.42	1.51	1.59	1.66
	62	1.99	1.18	1.38	1.51	1.62	1.70	1.78
	63	2.04	1.20	1.41	1.55	1.65	1.74	1.81
	64	2.11	1.25	1.47	1.61	1.72	1.81	1.89
	65	2.17	1.38	1.61	1.77	1.89	1.99	2.08
	66	2.25	1.56	1.83	2.01	2.14	2.26	2.35
	67	2.37	1.56	1.82	2.00	2.14	2.25	2.35
	68	2.57	1.62	1.90	2.09	2.23	2.35	2.45
	69	2.74	1.75	2.05	2.25	2.40	2.53	2.64
	70	2.96	1.72	2.02	2.22	2.37	2.49	2.60
	71	3.14	1.74	2.04	2.24	2.40	2.52	2.63
	72	3.31	1.95	2.28	2.51	2.68	2.82	2.94
Fabricated metal products	58	2.25	1.71	1.84	1.92	1.98	2.03	2.07
	59	2.35	1.86	2.00	2.09	2.15	2.21	2.25
	60	2.43	1.87	2.01	2.10	2.17	2.22	2.26
	61	2.49	1.89	2.03	2.12	2.19	2.24	2.29
	62	2.55	1.99	2.14	2.23	2.30	2.36	2.41
	63	2.61	2.04	2.19	2.29	2.36	2.42	2.47
	64	2.68	2.11	2.28	2.38	2.45	2.51	2.56
	65	2.76	2.26	2.43	2.54	2.62	2.68	2.74
	66	2.88	2.47	2.66	2.78	2.87	2.94	2.99
	67	2.98	2.51	2.71	2.83	2.91	2.98	3.04
	68	3.16	2.59	2.79	2.92	3.01	3.08	3.14
	69	3.34	2.77	2.99	3.12	3.22	3.29	3.36

Table A-4 (continued)

Industry	Year	Actual Wage	Estimated Personnel Costs per Recruit					
			$500	$1000	$1500	$2000	$2500	$3000
	70	3.53	2.82	3.04	3.18	3.28	3.36	3.42
	71	3.74	2.92	3.14	3.28	3.39	3.47	3.54
	72	3.99	3.19	3.44	3.59	3.70	3.79	3.87
Paper and paper products	58	2.10	1.62	1.74	1.82	1.87	1.92	1.96
	59	2.18	1.77	1.91	1.99	2.05	2.10	2.14
	60	2.26	1.78	1.91	2.00	2.06	2.11	2.15
	61	2.34	1.79	1.93	2.01	2.07	2.12	2.16
	62	2.40	1.90	2.04	2.13	2.19	2.24	2.29
	63	2.48	1.94	2.09	2.18	2.25	2.30	2.35
	64	2.56	2.02	2.17	2.27	2.34	2.39	2.44
	65	2.65	2.17	2.34	2.44	2.51	2.57	2.62
	66	2.75	2.40	2.58	2.69	2.77	2.84	2.89
	67	2.87	2.43	2.61	2.73	2.81	2.88	2.93
	68	3.05	2.51	2.70	2.82	2.91	2.98	3.03
	69	3.24	2.69	2.90	3.02	3.12	3.19	3.25
	70	3.44	2.73	2.93	3.06	3.15	3.23	3.29
	71	3.68	2.81	3.02	3.15	3.24	3.32	3.39
	72	3.94	3.08	3.32	3.46	3.57	3.65	3.72
Rubber and plastics	58	2.19	1.81	1.92	1.98	2.03	2.07	2.10
	59	2.27	1.92	2.03	2.10	2.15	2.19	2.23
	60	2.32	1.95	2.07	2.14	2.19	2.23	2.27
	61	2.38	1.99	2.10	2.18	2.23	2.27	2.31
	62	2.44	2.06	2.19	2.26	2.32	2.36	2.40

Year							
63	2.46	2.42	2.38	2.32	2.25	2.12	2.47
64	2.54	2.50	2.46	2.40	2.32	2.19	2.54
65	2.67	2.63	2.58	2.52	2.43	2.30	2.61
66	2.84	2.80	2.75	2.68	2.59	2.45	2.67
67	2.92	2.88	2.82	2.76	2.67	2.52	2.74
68	2.99	2.95	2.89	2.83	2.73	2.58	2.92
69	3.19	3.14	3.08	3.01	2.91	2.74	3.07
70	3.31	3.26	3.20	3.13	3.02	2.85	3.20
71	3.47	3.42	3.35	3.27	3.16	2.99	3.41
72	3.73	3.68	3.61	3.52	3.41	3.21	3.60

Furniture and fixtures

Year							
58	1.77	1.75	1.72	1.68	1.63	1.55	1.78
59	1.91	1.88	1.85	1.81	1.76	1.67	1.83
60	1.93	1.90	1.87	1.83	1.78	1.69	1.88
61	1.95	1.93	1.90	1.85	1.80	1.71	1.91
62	2.05	2.02	1.99	1.95	1.89	1.79	1.95
63	2.11	2.08	2.04	2.00	1.94	1.84	2.00
64	2.18	2.15	2.12	2.07	2.01	1.91	2.05
65	2.32	2.29	2.25	2.20	2.14	2.03	2.12
66	2.52	2.48	2.44	2.39	2.32	2.20	2.21
67	2.57	2.54	2.49	2.44	2.37	2.25	2.33
68	2.65	2.61	2.57	2.51	2.44	2.31	2.47
69	2.83	2.79	2.74	2.68	2.60	2.47	2.62
70	2.90	2.86	2.81	2.75	2.67	2.54	2.77
71	3.01	2.97	2.92	2.86	2.77	2.63	2.90
72	3.28	3.23	3.18	3.11	3.02	2.87	3.06

Stone, clay, and glass products

Year							
58	2.12	2.11	2.09	2.07	2.04	2.00	2.12
59	2.21	2.20	2.18	2.16	2.14	2.09	2.17
60	2.27	2.26	2.24	2.22	2.19	2.15	2.28
61	2.33	2.31	2.30	2.28	2.25	2.20	2.34

Table A-4 (continued)

Industry	Year	Actual Wage	Estimated Personnel Costs per Recruit					
			$500	$1000	$1500	$2000	$2500	$3000
	62	2.41	2.27	2.32	2.35	2.37	2.39	2.40
	63	2.47	2.33	2.39	2.42	2.44	2.46	2.47
	64	2.53	2.40	2.46	2.49	2.51	2.53	2.54
	65	2.62	2.49	2.55	2.58	2.61	2.62	2.64
	66	2.72	2.62	2.68	2.71	2.74	2.76	2.77
	67	2.82	2.71	2.77	2.81	2.83	2.85	2.87
	68	2.99	2.77	2.83	2.86	2.89	2.91	2.93
	69	3.19	2.93	3.00	3.04	3.07	3.09	3.11
	70	3.40	3.09	3.16	3.21	3.23	3.26	3.28
	71	3.66	3.27	3.34	3.39	3.42	3.44	3.46
	72	3.91	3.49	3.56	3.61	3.64	3.67	3.69
Primary metal products	58	2.64	2.30	2.38	2.43	2.47	2.50	2.52
	59	2.77	2.42	2.51	2.56	2.60	2.63	2.66
	60	2.81	2.48	2.57	2.62	2.66	2.69	2.72
	61	2.90	2.53	2.62	2.67	2.72	2.75	2.77
	62	2.98	2.62	2.72	2.78	2.82	2.85	2.88
	63	3.04	2.69	2.79	2.85	2.90	2.93	2.96
	64	3.11	2.78	2.88	2.94	2.98	3.02	3.05
	65	3.18	2.90	3.01	3.07	3.12	3.15	3.18
	66	3.28	3.07	3.19	3.26	3.30	3.34	3.38
	67	3.34	3.17	3.29	3.36	3.41	3.45	3.48
	68	3.55	3.24	3.36	3.43	3.49	3.53	3.56
	69	3.79	3.45	3.57	3.65	3.70	3.75	3.78
	70	3.93	3.61	3.74	3.82	3.88	3.92	3.96

	Year							
	71	4.23	3.79	3.93	4.01	4.08	4.12	4.16
	72	4.66	4.06	4.21	4.30	4.37	4.42	4.46
Electrical machinery	58	2.12	1.99	2.06	2.10	2.12	2.14	2.16
	59	2.20	2.08	2.15	2.19	2.22	2.24	2.26
	60	2.28	2.14	2.21	2.25	2.28	2.30	2.32
	61	2.35	2.19	2.26	2.30	2.33	2.35	2.37
	62	2.40	2.26	2.33	2.38	2.41	2.43	2.45
	63	2.46	2.32	2.40	2.44	2.47	2.50	2.52
	64	2.51	2.39	2.47	2.51	2.55	2.57	2.59
	65	2.58	2.48	2.56	2.61	2.64	2.67	2.69
	66	2.65	2.61	2.69	2.74	2.78	2.80	2.83
	67	2.77	2.70	2.79	2.84	2.87	2.90	2.93
	68	2.93	2.76	2.84	2.89	2.93	2.96	2.99
	69	3.09	2.92	3.01	3.07	3.11	3.14	3.17
	70	3.28	3.08	3.18	3.24	3.28	3.31	3.34
	71	3.50	3.25	3.36	3.42	3.46	3.50	3.53
	72	3.67	3.47	3.58	3.64	3.69	3.73	3.76
Instruments and related products	58	2.15	2.05	2.10	2.13	2.16	2.17	2.19
	59	2.24	2.15	2.20	2.23	2.26	2.27	2.29
	60	2.31	2.21	2.26	2.29	2.32	2.33	2.35
	61	2.38	2.26	2.31	2.35	2.37	2.39	2.40
	62	2.44	2.33	2.39	2.43	2.45	2.47	2.48
	63	2.49	2.40	2.46	2.49	2.52	2.54	2.55
	64	2.54	2.47	2.53	2.57	2.59	2.61	2.63
	65	2.62	2.57	2.63	2.67	2.69	2.72	2.73
	66	2.73	2.70	2.77	2.81	2.83	2.86	2.87
	67	2.85	2.80	2.86	2.90	2.93	2.96	2.98
	68	2.98	2.85	2.92	2.96	2.99	3.02	3.04
	69	3.15	3.03	3.10	3.14	3.18	3.20	3.22
	70	3.35	3.19	3.27	3.31	3.35	3.37	3.39

Table A-4 (continued)

Industry	Year	Actual Wage	Estimated Personnel Costs per Recruit					
			$500	$1000	$1500	$2000	$2500	$3000
	71	3.53	3.37	3.45	3.50	3.53	3.56	3.58
	72	3.72	3.59	3.68	3.73	3.77	3.80	3.82
Miscellaneous manufacturing industries	58	1.79	1.84	1.93	1.99	2.03	2.06	2.09
	59	1.84	1.94	2.04	2.10	2.14	2.18	2.21
	60	1.89	1.98	2.08	2.14	2.19	2.22	2.25
	61	1.92	2.02	2.12	2.18	2.23	2.26	2.29
	62	1.98	2.10	2.20	2.27	2.32	2.35	2.38
	63	2.03	2.16	2.26	2.33	2.38	2.42	2.45
	64	2.08	2.22	2.34	2.40	2.45	2.49	2.52
	65	2.14	2.33	2.45	2.52	2.57	2.61	2.64
	66	2.22	2.48	2.60	2.68	2.73	2.78	2.81
	67	2.35	2.55	2.68	2.76	2.81	2.86	2.90
	68	2.50	2.61	2.74	2.82	2.88	2.93	2.97
	69	2.66	2.78	2.92	3.00	3.06	3.11	3.15
	70	2.82	2.90	3.04	3.13	3.19	3.24	3.29
	71	2.96	3.04	3.19	3.28	3.35	3.40	3.45
	72	3.11	3.26	3.43	3.53	3.60	3.66	3.70
Tobacco and tobacco products	58	1.59	1.85	1.92	1.97	2.00	2.02	2.04
	59	1.64	1.93	2.00	2.05	2.08	2.11	2.13
	60	1.70	1.98	2.06	2.11	2.14	2.17	2.19
	61	1.78	2.03	2.11	2.15	2.19	2.22	2.24
	62	1.85	2.09	2.17	2.22	2.26	2.29	2.31
	63	1.91	2.15	2.23	2.28	2.32	2.35	2.37

64	2.44	2.42	2.39	2.35	2.30	2.21	1.95
65	2.53	2.50	2.47	2.43	2.38	2.29	2.09
66	2.65	2.62	2.59	2.55	2.49	2.40	2.19
67	2.75	2.72	2.69	2.64	2.58	2.49	2.27
68	2.80	2.77	2.74	2.69	2.63	2.53	2.48
69	2.97	2.94	2.90	2.86	2.79	2.69	2.62
70	3.13	3.10	3.06	3.01	2.95	2.83	2.92
71	3.31	3.28	3.24	3.19	3.11	3.00	3.15
72	3.52	3.49	3.45	3.39	3.32	3.19	3.43
Textile mill products							
58	1.67	1.65	1.62	1.59	1.54	1.46	1.49
59	1.78	1.76	1.73	1.69	1.64	1.55	1.56
60	1.81	1.79	1.76	1.72	1.67	1.58	1.61
61	1.84	1.82	1.78	1.75	1.69	1.61	1.63
62	1.92	1.89	1.86	1.82	1.77	1.67	1.68
63	1.97	1.94	1.91	1.87	1.81	1.72	1.71
64	2.04	2.01	1.97	1.93	1.87	1.78	1.79
65	2.14	2.11	2.08	2.03	1.97	1.87	1.87
66	2.30	2.26	2.23	2.18	2.11	2.00	1.96
67	2.36	2.32	2.28	2.24	2.17	2.06	2.06
68	2.42	2.38	2.34	2.29	2.22	2.11	2.21
69	2.57	2.54	2.50	2.44	2.37	2.25	2.34
70	2.67	2.63	2.59	2.53	2.46	2.33	2.45
71	2.79	2.75	2.70	2.65	2.57	2.43	2.57
72	3.01	2.97	2.92	2.86	2.77	2.63	2.73
Chemicals and allied products							
58	2.25	2.23	2.20	2.16	2.11	2.02	2.29
59	2.39	2.36	2.33	2.29	2.23	2.14	2.40
60	2.43	2.41	2.37	2.33	2.28	2.18	2.50
61	2.48	2.45	2.42	2.38	2.32	2.22	2.58
62	2.58	2.55	2.52	2.47	2.41	2.31	2.65
63	2.65	2.62	2.59	2.54	2.48	2.38	2.72

Table A-4 (continued)

Industry	Year	Actual Wage	Estimated Personnel Costs per Recruit					
			$500	$1000	$1500	$2000	$2500	$3000
	64	2.80	2.46	2.56	2.62	2.67	2.71	2.74
	65	2.89	2.58	2.69	2.76	2.80	2.84	2.87
	66	2.99	2.75	2.87	2.94	2.99	3.03	3.07
	67	3.10	2.83	2.95	3.02	3.08	3.12	3.15
	68	3.26	2.90	3.02	3.10	3.15	3.20	3.23
	69	3.47	3.09	3.22	3.30	3.36	3.40	3.44
	70	3.64	3.21	3.35	3.43	3.49	3.54	3.58
	71	3.94	3.36	3.51	3.59	3.66	3.71	3.75
	72	4.20	3.62	3.78	3.87	3.94	3.99	4.03
Leather and leather products	58	1.56	1.41	1.51	1.57	1.62	1.65	1.68
	59	1.59	1.50	1.60	1.66	1.71	1.75	1.78
	60	1.64	1.52	1.63	1.69	1.74	1.78	1.81
	61	1.68	1.55	1.66	1.72	1.77	1.81	1.84
	62	1.72	1.61	1.72	1.79	1.84	1.88	1.92
	63	1.76	1.65	1.77	1.84	1.89	1.93	1.97
	64	1.82	1.70	1.82	1.90	1.95	1.99	2.03
	65	1.88	1.79	1.91	1.99	2.05	2.09	2.13
	66	1.94	1.91	2.04	2.12	2.18	2.23	2.27
	67	2.07	1.96	2.09	2.18	2.24	2.29	2.33
	68	2.23	2.01	2.15	2.23	2.30	2.35	2.39
	69	2.36	2.13	2.28	2.37	2.44	2.49	2.54
	70	2.49	2.22	2.37	2.47	2.54	2.59	2.64
	71	2.59	2.32	2.48	2.58	2.66	2.72	2.76
	72	2.71	2.50	2.67	2.78	2.86	2.92	2.97

for the firm or industry. In a long-run model personnel costs could be a function of the other variables of the model rather than being an exogenous variable as in the short-run model used in this study.

In this study personnel costs are treated as exogenous[8] and optimal wage and quit rates are estimated. I have, however, used the model to calculate the level of personnel costs that would have to exist to rationalize existing wages as optimal. These are listed by industry and year in Table A-3. The objection might be raised that personnel costs are not stable but depend on layoffs. If the firm is laying off workers and reducing its work force, one might argue that it will not regard quits as a cost. But empirically most layoffs and rehirings occur because of seasonal variations in the demand for the final product. Most workers who are laid off are rehired, and most workers who quit are replaced. For this reason personnel costs will not be closely related to annual changes in layoffs, rehires, quits, or new hires.

A Presentation of Results

Using expressions (5) and (6), the actual values of Q_m and W_m (the quit and wage rates in all manufacturing industries) and estimates for the value of P (the value per employee of specific human capital), the optimal wage and quit rates are calculated for all nineteen industries and listed in Tables A-4 and A-5. I have used six estimates for the value of P in 1972, from $500 to $3,000 in increments of $500. The values of P for years previous to 1972 were calculated by deflating the 1972 dollars by the wholesale price index. This permits a calculation of the optimal wage in current dollars for each of the years 1958-1972.

From Table A-4, the deviations of optimal from actual wages were calculated for each of the nineteen industries, for each year, with each of the estimates of P, as a percentage of the actual wage. These deviations of optimal from actual wages are listed in Table A-6. The deviations may in some cases appear to reflect adversely on the performance of managers in various industries in maintaining wages at efficient levels. However, one must be cautious in applying these figures to individual businesses other than the Postal Service. Individual employers probably know what they are doing, all things considered, and it would be an inappropriate application of the results of this study to tell any individual employer that his wage rates are too high or too low by a specific amount. For industries other than the

---

[8] For an example of a model based on a similar approach, see Harry C. Benham, "Layoffs and Other Turnover Flows: Industry Differences and the Role of Fixed Employment Costs" (unpublished manuscript), December 1975.

Table A-5

OPTIMAL AND ACTUAL ANNUAL QUIT RATES

Industry	Year	Actual	Optimal					
			Estimated Personnel Costs per Recruit					
			$500	$1000	$1500	$2000	$2500	$3000
Postal Service	58	5.35	116.27	64.52	45.72	35.80	29.62	25.37
	59	6.89	130.87	72.62	51.46	40.30	33.34	28.55
	60	6.67	128.88	71.52	50.67	39.69	32.83	28.12
	61	6.09	129.35	71.78	50.86	39.83	32.95	28.22
	62	6.20	138.20	76.69	54.34	42.55	35.20	30.15
	63	5.03	142.09	78.85	55.87	43.75	36.19	31.00
	64	4.75	148.10	82.18	58.23	45.60	37.73	32.31
	65		159.99	88.78	62.91	49.26	40.76	34.91
	66		176.29	97.83	69.32	54.29	44.91	38.46
	67	12.39	175.69	97.49	69.08	54.10	44.76	38.33
	68	12.56	178.84	99.24	70.32	55.07	45.56	39.02
	69	13.42	185.91	103.17	73.10	57.25	47.36	40.56
	70	10.80	176.60	98.00	69.44	54.38	44.99	38.53
	71	6.21	173.20	96.11	68.10	53.33	44.12	37.79
	72	6.70	185.68	103.04	73.01	57.18	47.30	40.51
Machinery, except electrical	58	8.4	94.58	50.36	34.83	26.82	21.89	18.55
	59	13.2	101.34	53.96	37.32	28.73	23.46	19.87
	60	10.8	102.37	54.51	37.71	29.03	23.70	20.08
	61	9.6	104.31	55.54	38.42	29.58	24.14	20.46
	62	12.0	108.81	57.94	40.07	30.85	25.19	21.34

63	12.0	112.08	59.68	41.28	31.78	25.94	21.98
64	13.2	115.68	61.60	42.61	32.80	26.78	22.69
65	16.8	120.25	64.03	44.29	34.10	27.84	23.58
66	22.8	125.87	67.03	46.36	35.69	29.14	24.69
67	20.4	128.29	68.32	47.25	36.38	29.70	25.16
68	20.4	128.75	68.56	47.42	36.51	29.80	25.25
69	22.8	132.31	70.45	48.73	37.52	30.63	25.95
70	15.6	131.20	69.86	48.32	37.20	30.37	25.73
71	12.0	132.23	70.41	48.70	37.49	30.61	25.93
72	15.6	137.24	73.08	50.55	38.92	31.77	26.92

Transportation equipment

58	10.8	154.53	88.40	63.76	50.56	42.24	36.47
59	13.2	171.67	98.20	70.83	56.17	46.93	40.52
60	10.8	169.74	97.10	70.03	55.54	46.40	40.06
61	9.6	170.63	97.61	70.40	55.83	46.64	40.27
62	12.0	181.06	103.57	74.70	59.24	49.49	42.73
63	10.8	185.88	106.33	76.69	60.82	50.81	43.87
64	12.0	193.04	110.42	79.64	63.16	52.77	45.56
65	15.6	206.60	118.18	85.24	67.60	56.48	48.76
66	22.8	224.92	128.66	92.80	73.60	61.49	53.08
67	20.4	224.81	128.60	92.75	73.56	61.45	53.06
68	21.6	228.20	130.54	94.15	74.67	62.38	53.86
69	22.8	236.34	135.20	97.51	77.34	64.61	55.78
70	15.6	226.38	129.50	93.40	74.07	61.88	53.43
71	13.2	223.02	127.57	92.02	72.98	60.97	52.64
72	16.8	237.16	135.66	97.85	77.60	64.83	55.97

Apparel and other textile products

58	20.4	123.89	71.03	51.30	40.72	34.04	29.41
59	27.6	132.90	76.19	55.03	43.68	36.52	31.55
60	27.6	133.53	76.55	55.29	43.89	36.69	31.70
61	24.0	135.43	77.64	56.07	44.51	37.21	32.15

Table A-5 (continued)

Industry	Year	Actual	Optimal					
			Estimated Personnel Costs per Recruit					
			$500	$1000	$1500	$2000	$2500	$3000
	62	27.6	141.22	80.96	58.47	46.42	38.80	33.52
	63	26.4	144.97	83.11	60.02	47.65	39.83	34.41
	64	26.4	149.37	85.63	61.85	49.09	41.04	35.48
	65	31.2	155.66	89.24	64.45	51.16	42.77	36.95
	66	39.6	163.58	93.78	67.73	53.77	44.95	38.33
	67	34.8	165.75	95.03	68.63	54.48	45.55	39.35
	68	34.8	166.68	95.56	69.02	54.79	45.80	39.57
	69	37.2	171.13	98.11	70.86	56.25	47.03	40.62
	70	34.8	168.61	96.66	69.81	55.42	46.33	40.02
	71	33.6	169.00	96.89	69.97	55.55	46.44	40.12
	72	42.0	175.69	100.72	72.74	57.75	48.28	41.70
Ordnance and accessories	58	12.0	37.62	19.24	13.00	9.84	7.93	6.65
	59	20.4	39.28	20.09	13.57	10.27	8.28	6.94
	60	13.2	40.26	20.59	13.91	10.53	8.49	7.11
	61	13.2	41.40	21.17	14.30	10.83	8.73	7.31
	62	14.4	42.65	21.82	14.74	11.16	8.99	7.54
	63	12.0	44.02	22.52	15.21	11.51	9.28	7.78
	64	10.8	45.22	23.13	15.62	11.83	9.53	7.99
	65	13.2	46.05	23.55	15.91	12.04	9.71	8.14
	66	18.0	46.88	23.98	16.20	12.26	9.88	8.28
	67	20.4	48.42	24.76	16.73	12.67	10.21	8.56
	68	22.8	48.21	24.66	16.66	12.61	10.16	8.52

69	21.6	49.25	25.19	17.02	12.88	10.38	8.70
70	13.2	50.03	25.59	17.29	13.09	10.55	8.84
71	9.6	51.21	26.19	17.69	13.40	10.79	9.05
72	10.8	52.24	26.72	18.05	13.67	11.01	9.23

Lumber and wood products

58	20.4	150.22	88.03	64.40	51.58	43.43	37.73
59	31.2	167.97	98.43	72.00	57.68	48.56	42.19
60	27.6	165.32	96.88	70.87	56.77	47.80	41.53
61	28.8	165.68	97.09	71.02	56.89	47.90	41.62
62	32.4	176.32	103.32	75.58	60.54	50.97	44.29
63	33.6	180.81	105.95	77.51	62.09	52.27	45.42
64	40.8	187.92	110.12	80.56	64.53	54.33	47.20
65	54.0	202.22	118.50	86.69	69.44	58.46	50.80
66	49.2	221.80	129.98	95.08	76.17	64.13	55.72
67	50.4	220.74	129.35	94.62	75.80	63.82	55.45
68	54.0	224.59	131.61	96.27	77.12	64.93	56.41
69	39.6	232.88	136.47	99.83	79.97	67.33	58.50
70	37.2	221.49	129.80	94.95	76.06	64.04	55.64
71	46.8	217.16	127.26	93.09	74.57	62.78	54.55
72		231.96	135.93	99.43	79.65	67.06	58.27

Fabricated metal products

58	10.8	103.66	55.82	38.87	30.06	24.63	20.93
59	16.8	112.23	60.44	42.08	32.55	26.67	22.66
60	13.2	112.75	60.72	42.27	32.70	26.79	22.76
61	12.0	114.50	61.66	42.93	33.20	27.21	23.12
62	15.6	120.04	64.64	45.01	34.81	28.52	24.24
63	15.6	123.59	66.56	46.34	35.84	29.37	24.95
64	18.0	127.81	68.83	47.92	37.07	30.37	25.81
65	22.8	133.95	72.14	50.23	38.85	31.83	27.05
66	33.6	141.76	76.34	53.15	41.11	33.68	28.62
67	30.0	143.77	77.43	53.91	41.69	34.16	29.03

Table A-5 (continued)

Industry	Year	Actual	Optimal Estimated Personnel Costs per Recruit					
			$500	$1000	$1500	$2000	$2500	$3000
	68	33.6	144.73	77.94	54.27	41.97	34.39	29.22
	69	37.2	149.08	80.28	55.90	43.23	35.42	30.10
	70	25.2	146.47	78.88	54.92	42.48	34.80	29.57
	71	19.2	146.75	79.03	55.02	42.56	34.87	29.63
	72	25.2	153.36	82.59	57.50	44.48	36.44	30.97
Paper and paper products	58	10.8	95.81	51.51	35.83	27.69	22.68	19.26
	59	15.6	104.62	56.25	39.12	30.24	24.76	21.03
	60	14.4	104.70	56.29	39.15	30.26	24.78	21.05
	61	12.0	106.10	57.04	39.68	30.67	25.11	21.33
	62	13.2	111.71	60.06	41.77	32.29	26.44	22.46
	63	13.2	115.02	61.84	43.01	33.25	27.22	23.12
	64	15.6	119.18	64.08	44.57	34.45	28.21	23.96
	65	20.4	125.72	67.59	47.02	36.34	29.76	25.28
	66	28.8	134.19	72.15	50.18	38.79	31.76	26.98
	67	27.6	135.66	72.93	50.73	39.21	32.11	27.27
	68	30.0	136.87	73.58	51.18	39.56	32.40	27.52
	69	32.4	141.29	75.96	52.84	40.84	33.44	28.41
	70	24.0	137.87	74.13	51.56	39.85	32.63	27.72
	71	18.0	137.56	73.96	51.44	39.76	32.56	27.66
	72	20.4	144.56	77.72	54.06	41.78	34.22	29.06
Rubber and plastics	58	9.6	83.08	44.01	30.35	23.31	19.00	16.07
	59	15.6	87.81	46.52	32.08	24.64	20.08	16.99

60	14.4	89.30	47.31	32.62	25.06	20.42	17.28
61	14.4	91.34	48.38	33.36	25.63	20.89	17.67
62	18.0	94.64	50.13	34.57	26.56	21.64	18.31
63	16.8	97.51	51.66	35.62	27.36	22.30	18.87
64	18.0	100.35	53.16	36.66	28.16	22.95	19.42
65	25.2	103.23	54.68	37.71	28.97	23.61	19.97
66	37.2	106.55	56.44	38.92	29.90	24.37	20.62
67	34.8	109.23	57.86	39.90	30.65	24.98	21.13
68	37.2	109.20	57.85	39.89	30.64	24.97	21.13
69	43.2	111.85	59.25	40.86	31.39	25.58	21.64
70	31.2	112.19	59.43	40.98	31.48	25.66	21.71
71	24.0	113.88	60.33	41.60	31.96	26.04	22.04
72	33.6	117.15	62.06	42.79	32.87	26.79	22.67

Furniture and fixtures

58	15.6	63.30	33.33	22.91	17.55	14.28	12.06
59	22.8	68.08	35.85	24.64	18.88	15.36	12.97
60	20.4	68.71	36.18	24.86	19.05	15.50	13.09
61	18.0	69.98	36.85	25.33	19.41	15.79	13.34
62	25.2	73.15	38.52	26.47	20.29	16.50	13.94
63	25.2	75.39	39.70	27.28	20.91	17.01	14.37
64	28.8	77.90	41.02	28.19	21.60	17.57	14.84
65	37.2	81.19	42.76	29.38	22.52	18.32	15.47
66	51.6	85.28	44.91	30.86	23.65	19.24	16.25
67	44.4	86.86	45.74	31.43	24.09	19.59	16.55
68	49.2	87.23	45.94	31.57	24.19	19.68	16.62
69	54.0	89.74	47.26	32.48	24.89	20.24	17.10
70	38.4	88.79	46.76	32.13	24.62	20.03	16.92
71	36.0	89.39	47.07	32.35	24.79	20.16	17.03
72	49.2	92.99	48.97	33.65	25.79	20.98	17.72

Stone, clay, and glass products

58	12.0	33.32	17.03	11.50	8.70	7.01	5.88
59	16.8	34.72	17.75	11.98	9.07	7.31	6.12

Table A-5 (continued)

Industry	Year	Actual	\$500	\$1000	\$1500	\$2000	\$2500	\$3000
						Estimated Personnel Costs per Recruit (Optimal)		
	60	13.2	35.63	18.21	12.30	9.31	7.50	6.28
	61	12.0	36.65	18.73	12.65	9.57	7.71	6.46
	62	14.4	37.72	19.28	13.02	9.85	7.94	6.65
	63	14.4	38.93	19.90	13.44	10.17	8.19	6.87
	64	15.6	39.98	20.43	13.80	10.44	8.41	7.05
	65	20.4	40.64	20.77	14.03	10.62	8.55	7.17
	66	28.8	41.29	21.11	14.25	10.79	8.69	7.28
	67	27.6	42.68	21.82	14.73	11.15	8.98	7.53
	68	31.2	42.47	21.71	14.66	11.10	8.94	7.49
	69	36.0	43.37	22.17	14.97	11.33	9.13	7.65
	70	27.6	44.13	22.56	15.23	11.53	9.29	7.78
	71	22.8	45.22	23.12	15.61	11.81	9.52	7.98
	72	26.4	46.07	23.55	15.90	12.04	9.70	8.13
Primary metal products	58	4.8	63.78	33.06	22.51	17.14	13.87	11.67
	59	9.6	67.05	34.75	23.66	18.01	14.58	12.26
	60	7.2	68.45	35.48	24.16	18.39	14.88	12.52
	61	6.0	70.20	36.39	24.78	18.86	15.26	12.84
	62	7.2	72.56	37.61	25.61	19.50	15.78	13.27
	63	7.2	74.84	38.79	26.41	20.11	16.27	13.69
	64	10.8	76.97	39.90	27.16	20.68	16.74	14.08
	65	14.4	78.81	40.85	27.81	21.17	17.14	14.42
	66	20.4	80.83	41.90	28.53	21.72	17.58	14.79

	Year							
	67	16.8	83.17	43.11	29.35	22.35	18.09	15.21
	68	20.4	82.99	43.02	29.29	22.30	18.05	15.18
	69	24.0	84.91	44.02	29.97	22.82	18.46	15.53
	70	16.8	85.69	44.42	30.24	23.02	18.63	15.68
	71	12.0	87.34	45.28	30.83	23.47	18.99	15.98
	72	13.2	89.51	46.40	31.59	24.05	19.47	16.38
Electrical machinery	58	12.0	47.33	24.41	16.57	12.59	10.17	8.54
	59	16.8	49.33	25.44	17.27	13.12	10.60	8.91
	60	14.4	50.58	26.09	17.71	13.45	10.87	9.13
	61	14.4	52.00	26.82	18.21	13.83	11.18	9.39
	62	16.8	53.52	27.61	18.74	14.24	11.50	9.66
	63	15.6	55.22	28.48	19.33	14.69	11.87	9.97
	64	14.4	56.69	29.24	19.85	15.08	12.18	10.24
	65	19.2	57.66	29.74	20.19	15.34	12.39	10.41
	66	27.6	58.62	30.24	20.53	15.59	12.60	10.58
	67	24.0	60.55	31.23	21.20	16.11	13.01	10.93
	68	24.0	60.27	31.08	21.10	16.03	12.95	10.88
	69	27.6	61.54	31.74	21.55	16.37	13.23	11.11
	70	20.4	62.56	32.27	21.90	16.64	13.45	11.30
	71	14.4	64.06	33.04	22.43	17.04	13.77	11.57
	72	20.4	65.28	33.67	22.86	17.37	14.03	11.79
Instruments and related products	58	9.6	37.34	19.12	12.93	9.79	7.89	6.62
	59	15.6	38.97	19.96	13.49	10.22	8.24	6.91
	60	13.2	39.96	20.46	13.83	10.48	8.45	7.08
	61	12.0	41.08	21.04	14.22	10.77	8.68	7.28
	62	14.4	42.32	21.67	14.65	11.10	8.95	7.50
	63	14.4	43.67	22.37	15.12	11.45	9.23	7.74
	64	14.4	44.85	22.97	15.53	11.76	9.48	7.95
	65	16.8	45.66	23.39	15.81	11.98	9.65	8.10

Table A-5 (continued)

Industry	Year	Actual	Optimal					
			Estimated Personnel Costs per Recruit					
			$500	$1000	$1500	$2000	$2500	$3000
	66	22.8	46.48	23.80	16.09	12.19	9.83	8.24
	67	21.6	48.00	24.58	16.62	12.59	10.15	8.51
	68	21.6	47.79	24.47	16.55	12.53	10.10	8.47
	69	24.0	48.82	25.00	16.90	12.80	10.32	8.66
	70	18.0	49.60	25.40	17.17	13.01	10.49	8.79
	71	14.4	50.78	26.01	17.58	13.32	10.74	9.00
	72	19.2	51.79	26.52	17.93	13.58	10.95	9.18
Miscellaneous manufacturing industries	58	15.6	70.57	37.05	25.42	19.45	15.81	13.34
	59	22.8	74.43	39.08	26.81	20.52	16.67	14.07
	60	22.8	75.81	39.81	27.31	20.90	16.98	14.34
	61	21.6	77.62	40.76	27.96	21.40	17.39	14.68
	62	24.0	80.35	42.19	28.94	22.15	18.00	15.19
	63	21.6	82.83	43.49	29.83	22.83	18.56	15.66
	64	24.0	85.21	44.74	30.69	23.49	19.09	16.11
	65	31.2	87.50	45.94	31.52	24.12	19.60	16.55
	66	43.2	90.09	47.30	32.45	24.84	20.18	17.04
	67	38.4	92.49	48.57	33.32	25.50	20.72	17.49
	68	39.6	92.40	48.52	33.28	25.47	20.70	17.47
	69	43.2	94.60	49.67	34.08	26.08	21.19	17.89
	70	34.8	95.12	49.94	34.26	26.22	21.31	17.99
	71	28.8	96.71	50.78	34.83	26.66	21.67	18.29
	72	36.0	99.34	52.16	35.78	27.39	22.26	18.79

Tobacco and tobacco products

58	12.0	55.10	28.63	19.52	14.88	12.05	10.14
59	13.2	57.29	29.77	20.30	15.47	12.53	10.55
60	12.0	58.78	30.54	20.83	15.87	12.85	10.82
61	10.8	60.44	31.41	21.42	16.30	13.22	11.13
62	10.8	62.13	32.29	22.01	16.75	13.59	11.44
63	10.8	64.08	33.30	22.70	17.30	14.01	11.80
64	15.6	65.73	34.16	23.29	17.75	14.38	12.10
65	18.0	66.74	34.68	23.65	18.02	14.60	12.29
66	22.8	67.70	35.18	23.99	18.28	14.81	12.46
67	25.2	69.96	36.35	24.79	18.89	15.30	12.88
68	25.2	69.60	36.17	24.66	18.79	15.22	12.81
69	27.6	71.02	36.90	25.16	19.18	15.53	13.07
70	24.0	72.29	37.57	25.62	19.52	15.81	13.31
71	19.2	74.08	38.50	26.25	20.00	16.20	13.64
72	20.4	75.39	39.17	26.71	20.36	16.49	13.88

Textile mill products

58	15.6	60.50	31.88	21.91	16.80	13.66	11.54
59	20.4	64.23	33.84	23.27	17.83	14.51	12.26
60	19.2	65.21	34.36	23.62	18.10	14.73	12.44
61	19.2	66.64	35.11	24.14	18.50	15.05	12.72
62	22.8	69.20	36.47	25.07	19.21	15.63	13.21
63	22.8	71.32	37.58	25.84	19.80	16.11	13.61
64	25.2	73.48	38.72	26.62	20.40	16.60	14.02
65	30.0	75.83	39.96	27.47	21.06	17.13	14.47
66	42.0	78.61	41.42	28.48	21.83	17.76	15.00
67	40.8	80.48	42.44	29.15	22.35	18.18	15.36
68	43.2	80.55	42.41	29.18	22.36	18.20	15.37
69	46.8	82.60	43.52	29.92	22.93	18.66	15.76
70	42.0	82.58	43.52	29.91	22.93	18.66	15.76
71	40.8	83.67	44.09	30.31	23.23	18.90	15.97
72	50.4	86.32	45.48	31.27	23.97	19.50	16.47

Table A-5 (continued)

Industry	Year	Actual	Optimal — Estimated Personnel Costs per Recruit					
			$500	$1000	$1500	$2000	$2500	$3000
Chemicals and allied products	58	7.2	65.27	34.02	23.24	17.73	14.38	12.11
	59	9.6	69.09	36.01	24.60	18.77	15.22	12.82
	60	9.6	70.29	36.64	25.03	19.10	15.48	13.04
	61	8.4	71.93	37.50	25.61	19.54	15.85	13.35
	62	9.6	74.60	38.89	26.56	20.27	16.43	13.84
	63	9.6	76.93	40.10	27.39	20.90	16.95	14.28
	64	9.6	79.22	41.29	28.21	21.52	17.45	14.70
	65	12.0	81.55	42.51	29.04	22.16	17.86	15.13
	66	16.8	84.24	43.91	30.00	22.89	18.56	15.63
	67	15.6	86.41	45.04	30.77	23.48	19.04	16.04
	68	18.0	86.39	45.03	30.76	23.47	19.03	16.03
	69	19.2	88.54	46.15	31.53	24.06	19.50	16.43
	70	14.4	88.82	46.30	31.63	24.13	19.57	16.48
	71	10.8	90.19	47.01	32.11	24.50	19.87	16.74
	72	12.0	92.85	48.40	33.06	25.23	20.45	17.23
Leather and leather products	58	19.2	76.43	40.86	28.33	21.84	17.86	15.14
	59	26.4	80.70	43.14	29.91	23.06	18.85	15.99
	60	26.4	82.06	43.87	30.41	23.45	19.17	16.26
	61	24.0	83.91	44.86	31.10	23.98	19.60	16.62
	62	27.6	86.88	46.45	32.20	24.83	20.30	17.21
	63	27.6	89.48	47.84	33.17	25.58	20.91	17.73
	64	28.8	92.04	49.21	34.11	26.31	21.50	18.24

65	36.0	94.62	50.59	35.07	27.04	22.11	18.75
66	49.2	97.59	52.18	36.17	27.89	22.80	19.34
67	43.2	100.02	53.47	37.07	28.59	23.37	19.82
68	46.8	99.99	53.46	37.06	28.58	23.36	19.81
69	48.0	102.37	54.73	37.94	29.26	23.92	20.28
70	42.0	102.70	54.91	38.07	29.35	23.99	20.35
71	37.2	104.24	55.73	38.64	29.79	24.35	20.65
72	49.2	107.17	57.30	39.72	30.63	25.04	21.24

Table A-6

PERCENT DEVIATIONS OF OPTIMAL FROM ACTUAL WAGES

Industry	Year	Estimated Personnel Costs per Recruit					
		$500	$1000	$1500	$2000	$2500	$3000
Postal Service	58	45.43	39.44	35.64	32.79	30.50	28.56
	59	38.69	31.95	27.67	24.47	21.90	19.73
	60	39.79	33.18	28.98	25.84	23.31	21.18
	61	44.91	38.85	35.01	32.14	29.82	27.87
	62	40.69	34.17	30.04	26.94	24.45	22.35
	63	44.15	38.02	34.12	31.21	28.86	26.89
	64	43.04	36.79	32.81	29.84	27.45	25.43
	65	40.49	33.96	29.80	26.70	24.20	22.09
	66	34.58	27.40	22.83	19.42	16.67	14.35
	67	36.05	29.03	24.57	21.23	18.54	16.28
	68	36.77	29.83	25.41	22.12	19.46	17.22
	69	35.50	28.42	23.92	20.55	17.84	15.56
	70	42.62	36.32	32.31	29.32	26.91	24.88
	71	48.14	42.44	38.82	36.12	33.94	32.10
	72	45.24	39.23	35.41	32.55	30.25	28.31
Machinery, except electrical	58	20.78	15.62	12.46	10.14	8.30	6.76
	59	18.68	13.39	10.14	7.75	5.86	4.29
	60	20.00	14.80	11.60	9.26	7.40	5.85
	61	21.06	15.93	12.77	10.46	8.63	7.10
	62	20.09	14.90	11.70	9.36	7.50	5.96
	63	20.06	14.86	11.67	9.33	7.47	5.92
	64	19.88	14.67	11.47	9.12	7.26	5.71

65	17.62	12.27	8.97	6.56	4.65	3.05
66	14.65	9.10	5.69	3.19	1.21	0.44
67	15.54	10.04	6.67	4.19	2.23	0.60
68	17.51	12.15	8.85	6.43	4.52	2.92
69	17.39	12.02	8.72	6.30	4.38	2.78
70	19.34	14.10	10.87	8.51	6.63	5.07
71	20.79	15.64	12.47	10.15	8.31	6.78
72	19.64	14.41	11.20	8.85	6.98	5.42
Transportation equipment						
58	49.29	41.98	37.23	33.62	30.68	28.18
59	46.30	38.56	33.53	29.71	26.60	23.95
60	48.78	41.40	36.59	32.95	29.98	27.46
61	49.86	42.64	37.94	34.37	31.47	29.00
62	48.62	41.21	36.40	32.74	29.77	27.24
63	49.19	41.87	37.11	33.50	30.55	28.05
64	48.47	41.05	36.22	32.56	29.57	27.03
65	45.85	38.05	32.97	29.12	25.98	23.31
66	41.28	32.82	27.32	23.14	19.74	16.84
67	43.05	34.84	29.51	25.46	22.15	19.35
68	44.76	36.80	31.62	27.69	24.49	21.77
69	43.65	35.53	30.25	26.24	22.97	20.20
70	46.38	38.65	33.63	29.81	26.70	24.06
71	50.18	43.00	38.34	34.79	31.90	29.45
72	47.98	40.49	35.61	31.91	28.90	26.34
Apparel and other textile products						
58	35.08	25.55	19.35	14.64	10.79	7.53
59	31.08	20.97	14.39	9.38	5.30	1.83
60	31.98	22.00	15.50	10.56	6.53	3.10
61	33.44	23.68	17.32	12.49	8.55	5.20
62	32.40	22.48	16.02	11.11	7.11	3.71
63	32.46	22.56	16.10	11.20	7.20	3.80

153

Table A-6 (continued)

Industry	Year		Estimated Personnel Costs per Recruit				
		$500	$1000	$1500	$2000	$2500	$3000
	64	32.58	22.69	16.25	11.35	7.36	3.96
	65	29.89	19.61	12.91	7.81	3.67	0.14
	66	26.29	15.48	8.43	3.08	-1.28	-4.99
	67	30.29	20.07	13.41	8.35	4.22	0.71
	68	34.00	24.32	18.01	13.22	9.31	5.99
	69	32.68	22.81	16.38	11.50	7.51	4.12
	70	33.53	23.79	17.43	12.61	8.67	5.33
	71	34.06	24.38	18.08	13.30	9.39	6.07
	72	31.59	21.55	15.01	10.05	6.00	2.55
Ordnance and accessories	58	12.48	10.47	9.26	8.40	7.72	7.17
	59	10.53	8.47	7.24	6.36	5.67	5.10
	60	10.94	8.89	7.67	6.79	6.10	5.54
	61	12.21	10.18	8.98	8.12	7.44	6.88
	62	11.77	9.74	8.53	7.66	6.98	6.42
	63	12.38	10.36	9.16	8.30	7.62	7.07
	64	12.75	10.74	9.54	8.68	8.01	7.45
	65	12.26	10.24	9.03	8.17	7.49	6.93
	66	8.86	6.76	5.51	4.61	3.91	3.33
	67	5.94	3.78	2.49	1.56	0.83	0.24
	68	6.37	4.21	2.92	2.00	1.28	0.69
	69	5.32	3.14	1.83	0.90	0.17	-0.42
	70	5.53	3.35	2.05	1.12	0.39	-0.20
	71	6.49	4.33	3.04	2.12	1.40	0.81
	72	6.06	3.89	2.61	1.68	0.96	0.36

Lumber and wood products

Year						
58	43.90	34.25	27.86	22.94	18.91	15.45
59	39.81	29.45	22.59	17.32	12.99	9.28
60	41.31	31.22	24.52	19.39	15.16	11.54
61	43.28	33.52	27.06	22.09	18.01	14.51
62	40.63	30.42	23.65	18.45	14.17	10.51
63	40.83	30.65	23.91	18.73	14.47	10.82
64	40.39	30.14	23.35	18.13	13.83	10.16
65	36.38	25.43	18.18	12.61	8.03	4.11
66	30.46	18.50	10.56	4.48	−0.52	−4.81
67	34.14	22.81	15.30	9.54	4.79	0.73
68	36.66	25.77	18.54	13.00	8.43	4.53
69	36.04	25.03	17.74	12.14	7.53	3.59
70	41.60	31.56	24.90	19.79	15.58	11.98
71	44.34	34.77	28.42	23.55	19.54	16.11
72	41.01	30.86	24.13	18.96	14.72	11.08

Fabricated metal products

Year						
58	23.78	17.91	14.26	11.58	9.44	7.65
59	20.80	14.69	10.90	8.11	5.89	4.03
60	22.95	17.01	13.32	10.61	8.45	6.65
61	24.02	18.17	14.53	11.86	9.73	7.95
62	21.93	15.91	12.18	9.43	7.23	5.41
63	21.76	15.73	11.99	9.24	7.04	5.21
64	21.01	14.92	11.14	8.36	6.14	4.29
65	17.99	11.67	7.75	4.86	2.56	0.64
66	14.06	7.44	3.32	0.30	−2.10	−4.12
67	15.56	9.05	5.02	2.04	−0.32	−2.30
68	17.84	11.50	7.58	4.68	2.38	0.45
69	16.86	10.45	6.47	3.55	1.21	−0.73
70	19.86	13.68	9.85	7.03	4.78	2.90
71	21.85	15.82	12.08	9.33	7.14	5.31
72	19.92	13.74	9.91	7.09	4.85	2.97

Table A-6 (continued)

Industry	Year	$500	$1000	$1500	$2000	$2500	$3000
				Estimated Personnel Costs per Recruit			
Paper and paper products	58	22.59	16.76	13.15	10.495	8.38	6.61
	59	18.37	12.22	8.41	5.614	3.38	1.51
	60	21.10	15.15	11.47	8.769	6.61	4.81
	61	23.16	17.38	13.79	11.158	9.05	7.30
	62	20.82	14.86	11.17	8.454	6.29	4.48
	63	21.40	15.48	11.82	9.125	6.97	5.18
	64	20.91	14.95	11.26	8.550	6.39	4.58
	65	17.78	11.59	7.75	4.935	2.68	0.81
	66	12.62	6.04	1.96	−1.036	−3.42	−5.41
	67	15.15	8.77	4.81	1.899	−0.42	−2.35
	68	17.43	11.22	7.37	4.537	2.27	0.39
	69	16.69	10.42	6.53	3.675	1.39	−0.50
	70	20.60	14.63	10.92	8.200	6.03	4.21
	71	23.63	17.88	14.32	11.701	9.61	7.87
	72	21.59	15.69	12.03	9.347	7.20	5.41
Rubber and plastics	58	17.24	12.31	9.30	7.10	5.35	3.90
	59	15.40	10.36	7.28	5.03	3.24	1.76
	60	15.71	10.69	7.62	5.38	3.60	2.12
	61	16.38	11.41	8.36	6.13	4.37	2.91
	62	15.17	10.12	7.03	4.77	2.98	1.50
	63	13.98	8.86	5.73	3.44	1.62	0.12
	64	13.70	8.57	5.42	3.12	1.31	−0.20
	65	11.87	6.63	3.42	1.07	−0.78	−2.32
	66	8.12	2.65	−0.69	−3.13	−5.07	−6.68

	(1)	(2)	(3)	(4)	(5)	(6)
67	8.00	2.52	−0.82	−3.27	−5.21	−6.82
68	11.53	6.27	3.04	0.69	−1.17	−2.72
69	10.51	5.18	1.92	−0.45	−2.33	−3.90
70	10.71	5.39	2.14	−0.23	−2.11	−3.68
71	12.28	7.06	3.87	1.53	−0.31	−1.85
72	10.59	5.27	2.01	−0.36	−2.25	−3.81

Furniture and fixtures

	(1)	(2)	(3)	(4)	(5)	(6)
58	12.84	8.20	5.37	3.30	1.67	0.32
59	8.59	3.72	0.75	−1.40	−3.12	−4.54
60	10.09	5.30	2.38	0.25	−1.42	−2.82
61	10.31	5.53	2.62	0.50	−1.17	−2.56
62	7.83	2.92	−0.07	−2.25	−3.97	−5.40
63	7.73	2.81	−0.18	−2.36	−4.09	−5.52
64	6.76	1.79	−1.24	−3.44	−5.19	−6.63
65	4.13	−0.97	−4.09	−6.35	−8.15	−9.64
66	0.19	−5.12	−8.37	10.73	12.59	14.14
67	3.34	−1.80	−4.94	−7.23	−9.03	10.53
68	6.14	1.14	−1.90	−4.12	−5.88	−7.34
69	5.48	0.44	−2.62	−4.86	−6.62	−8.09
70	8.28	3.39	0.41	−1.75	−3.47	−4.89
71	9.04	4.20	1.24	−0.90	−2.60	−4.02
72	6.19	1.19	−1.84	−4.06	−5.82	−7.27

Stone, clay, and glass products

	(1)	(2)	(3)	(4)	(5)	(6)
58	5.43	3.32	2.06	1.15	0.45	−0.13
59	3.50	1.34	0.05	−0.87	−1.58	−2.18
60	5.64	3.52	2.26	1.36	0.66	0.07
61	5.89	3.78	2.53	1.63	0.93	0.35
62	5.59	3.48	2.22	1.32	0.61	0.03
63	5.29	3.17	1.90	1.00	0.29	−0.28
64	4.82	2.69	1.42	0.51	−0.19	−0.78
65	4.67	2.54	1.27	0.36	−0.35	−0.93

Table A-6 (continued)

Industry	Year		Estimated Personnel Costs per Recruit				
		$500	$1000	$1500	$2000	$2500	$3000
	66	3.61	1.45	0.16	−0.75	−1.47	−2.06
	67	3.67	1.51	0.23	0.69	−1.41	−2.00
	68	7.33	5.26	4.02	3.13	2.44	1.87
	69	7.90	5.84	4.61	3.73	3.04	2.47
	70	8.83	6.79	5.57	4.70	4.02	3.46
	71	10.50	8.50	7.30	6.45	5.78	5.22
	72	10.71	8.71	7.52	6.67	6.00	5.46
Primary metal	58	12.80	9.59	7.66	6.26	5.17	4.26
products	59	12.41	9.19	7.25	5.85	4.75	3.84
	60	11.74	8.49	6.54	5.12	4.01	3.10
	61	12.73	9.52	7.59	6.20	5.10	4.19
	62	11.89	8.65	6.70	5.29	4.18	3.26
	63	11.25	7.99	6.02	4.60	3.48	2.56
	64	10.56	7.27	5.29	3.86	2.73	1.80
	65	8.64	5.27	3.25	1.79	0.64	−0.30
	66	6.12	2.67	0.59	−0.90	−2.08	−3.06
	67	4.91	1.41	−0.68	−2.20	−3.40	−4.39
	68	8.50	5.14	3.11	1.65	0.50	−0.45
	69	8.95	5.60	3.58	2.12	0.98	0.03
	70	8.12	4.74	2.70	1.23	0.07	−0.87
	71	10.26	6.96	4.98	3.54	2.41	1.48
	72	12.68	9.47	7.53	6.13	5.04	4.13

Electrical machinery						
58	5.70	2.72	0.93	−0.34	−1.35	−2.18
59	5.05	2.05	0.25	−1.04	−2.05	−2.90
60	5.94	2.97	1.19	−0.09	−1.10	−1.92
61	6.65	3.70	1.93	0.66	−0.33	−1.16
62	5.56	2.57	0.79	−0.50	−1.51	−2.34
63	5.30	2.31	0.52	−0.77	−1.78	−2.62
64	4.48	1.46	−0.34	−1.64	−2.66	−3.51
65	3.58	0.53	−1.29	−2.61	−3.64	−4.49
66	1.38	−1.73	−3.60	−4.94	−6.00	−6.87
67	2.82	−0.76	−2.61	−3.94	−4.99	−5.85
68	5.18	2.81	1.02	−0.25	−1.26	−2.10
69	5.28	2.28	0.49	−0.79	−1.81	−2.65
70	5.94	2.97	1.19	−0.09	−1.09	−1.92
71	6.92	3.98	2.22	0.94	−0.04	−0.86
72	5.37	2.38	0.58	−0.70	−1.71	−2.55
Instruments and related products						
58	4.21	1.88	0.49	−0.50	−1.28	−1.93
59	3.80	1.46	0.06	−0.93	−1.72	−2.37
60	4.25	1.92	0.52	−0.47	−1.25	−1.89
61	4.93	2.61	1.23	0.24	−0.53	−1.17
62	4.11	1.78	0.38	−0.61	−1.39	−2.04
63	3.40	1.04	−0.35	−1.36	−2.15	−2.80
64	2.49	0.11	−1.29	−2.31	−3.11	−3.76
65	1.82	−0.56	−1.99	−3.01	−3.81	−4.47
66	0.91	−1.49	−2.93	−3.97	−4.78	−5.44
67	1.74	−0.65	−2.08	−3.10	−3.91	−4.57
68	4.10	1.76	0.37	−0.62	−1.41	−2.05
69	3.76	1.42	0.02	−0.98	−1.76	−2.41
70	4.67	2.35	0.96	−0.02	−0.80	−1.44
71	4.49	2.16	0.77	−0.22	−1.00	−1.64
72	3.30	0.94	−0.45	−1.46	−2.25	−2.90

Table A-6 (continued)

Industry	Year	Estimated Personnel Costs per Recruit					
		$500	$1000	$1500	$2000	$2500	$3000
Miscellaneous manufacturing industries	58	−2.97	−8.14	−11.28	−13.56	−15.37	−16.86
	59	−5.92	−11.23	−14.47	−16.82	−18.67	−20.21
	60	−5.16	−10.44	−13.65	−15.98	−17.83	−19.35
	61	−5.46	−10.75	−13.97	−16.31	−18.16	−19.69
	62	−6.26	−11.60	−14.84	−17.19	−19.06	−20.60
	63	−6.43	−11.77	−15.02	−17.38	−19.25	−20.79
	64	−7.14	−12.51	−15.78	−18.16	−20.04	−21.60
	65	−9.08	−14.55	−17.88	−20.30	−22.21	−23.79
	66	−11.87	−17.48	−20.90	−23.38	−25.34	−26.96
	67	−8.76	−14.22	−17.53	−19.94	−21.85	−23.43
	68	−4.68	−9.94	−13.13	−15.45	−17.28	−18.80
	69	−4.59	−9.84	−13.03	−15.35	−17.18	−18.70
	70	−2.86	−8.02	−11.15	−13.44	−15.24	−16.73
	71	−2.75	−7.90	−11.04	−13.32	−15.12	−16.61
	72	−5.08	−10.35	−13.55	−15.89	−17.73	−19.25
Tobacco and tobacco products	58	−16.60	−21.19	−23.96	−25.96	−27.54	−28.84
	59	−17.82	−22.46	−25.26	−27.29	−28.88	−30.19
	60	−16.77	−21.37	−24.14	−28.15	−27.72	−29.03
	61	−14.10	−18.60	−21.30	−23.26	−24.80	−26.08
	62	−13.28	−17.74	−20.43	−22.37	−23.91	−25.17
	63	−12.73	−17.17	−19.84	−21.78	−23.30	−24.57
	64	−13.55	−18.02	−20.72	−22.67	−24.21	−25.47
	65	−9.74	−14.06	−16.67	−18.55	−20.04	−21.26
	66	−9.77	−14.10	−16.70	−18.59	−20.07	−21.30

	1	2	3	4	5	6
67	—9.69	—14.01	—16.62	—18.50	—19.98	—21.21
68	—2.39	—6.42	—8.85	—10.61	—11.99	—13.14
69	—2.68	—6.72	—9.16	—10.93	—12.31	—13.46
70	2.74	—1.08	—3.39	—5.06	—6.38	—7.46
71	4.72	0.97	—1.28	—2.92	—4.21	—5.27
72	6.86	3.19	0.98	—0.61	—1.87	—2.90

Textile mill
products

	1	2	3	4	5	6
58	1.70	—3.59	—6.82	—9.18	—11.04	—12.59
59	0.07	—5.31	—8.60	—10.99	—12.89	—14.46
60	1.58	—3.72	—6.96	—9.32	—11.18	—12.73
61	1.15	—4.17	—7.42	—9.79	—11.66	—13.22
62	0.02	—5.36	—8.65	—11.04	—12.94	—14.51
63	—0.84	—6.28	—9.60	—12.01	—13.92	—15.51
64	0.49	—4.87	—8.13	—10.52	—12.40	—13.97
65	—0.27	—5.68	—8.98	—11.38	—13.28	—14.86
66	—2.47	—8.01	—11.37	—13.83	—15.77	—17.38
67	—0.05	—5.45	—8.74	—11.14	—13.03	—14.61
68	4.32	—0.83	—3.98	—6.27	—8.09	—9.59
69	3.78	—1.40	—4.56	—6.87	—8.69	—10.20
70	4.73	—0.40	—3.54	—5.82	—7.62	—9.12
71	5.10	—0.01	—3.13	—5.40	—7.20	—8.69
72	3.59	—1.60	—4.77	—7.08	—8.90	—10.42

Chemicals and
allied products

	1	2	3	4	5	6
58	11.58	7.82	5.54	3.89	2.59	1.52
59	10.48	6.67	4.36	2.70	1.38	0.29
60	12.46	8.73	6.48	4.84	3.56	2.50
61	13.62	9.94	7.72	6.11	4.84	3.79
62	12.46	8.73	6.47	4.84	3.56	2.49
63	12.38	8.65	6.40	4.76	3.48	2.41
64	12.13	8.38	6.12	4.48	3.20	2.13
65	10.60	6.79	4.49	2.82	1.51	0.42

161

Table A-6 (continued)

Industry	Year		Estimated Personnel Costs per Recruit				
		$500	$1000	$1500	$2000	$2500	$3000
	66	7.76	3.83	1.46	−0.25	−1.60	−2.72
	67	8.52	4.63	2.28	0.57	−0.77	−1.88
	68	10.86	7.07	4.77	3.11	1.80	0.72
	69	10.88	7.09	4.80	3.13	1.83	0.74
	70	11.63	7.87	5.60	3.95	2.65	1.58
	71	14.51	10.87	8.67	7.07	5.82	4.78
	72	13.64	9.96	7.74	6.13	4.86	3.81
Leather and leather products	58	9.10	2.80	−1.08	−3.92	−6.19	−8.08
	59	5.60	−0.94	−4.97	−7.93	−10.28	−12.25
	60	6.82	0.36	−3.61	−6.53	−8.85	−10.79
	61	7.45	1.04	−2.91	−5.80	−8.11	−10.04
	62	6.04	−0.45	−4.47	−7.42	−9.76	−11.71
	63	5.78	−0.73	−4.76	−7.71	−10.06	−12.02
	64	6.06	−0.45	−4.46	−7.41	−9.75	−11.70
	65	4.62	−1.98	−6.05	−9.04	−11.42	−13.40
	66	1.50	−5.32	−9.53	−12.62	−15.08	−17.12
	67	5.15	−1.41	−5.46	−8.43	−10.80	−12.77
	68	9.79	3.54	−0.31	−3.14	−5.39	−7.26
	69	9.38	3.11	−0.76	−3.60	−5.86	−7.74
	70	10.65	4.46	0.65	−2.14	−4.37	−6.23
	71	10.09	3.86	0.02	−2.79	−5.03	−6.90
	72	7.59	1.19	−2.75	−5.65	−7.95	−9.87

Postal Service the data are highly aggregated at the two-digit level, so should not be specifically applied to industries producing quite different products, using different technologies, and hiring workers under different labor market conditions. Treating diverse industries under the same rubric may account for some of the statistical insignificance in the estimation of the parameters in the quit–wage rate relationship in Table A-1. For these reasons the results here calculated for two-digit industries should be regarded with considerable caution and used only for a rough comparison with the Postal Service. For more refined purposes, examining the industries at a more disaggregated level would be necessary.

Since wage contracts and downward rigidity of nominal wages introduce inflexibilities into the wage-determination process, it may not be possible for all managers to adjust their wages to optimal levels in any given year. For this reason positive or negative deviations in any given year should not be interpreted as indicating inefficient management. To provide a measure of the tendency of wages over a longer period, the means of the deviations are calculated for each of the nineteen industries over the period 1958-1972 for each of the estimates of specific human capital. These means are tabulated in Table A-7.

The personnel costs incurred by firms among different industries vary with the level of skill or expertise of the work force and this in turn is related to wages. As a first approximation, the level of wages can be used as an indicator of the level of personnel costs by industry. The mean levels of wages over the period 1958-1972 are listed by industry in column 1 of Table 12. To use wage levels as a tool for assigning P-values to industries, the difference between the highest and lowest wage was divided into six equal parts which were associated in consecutive order with the six P-values from $500 to $3,000. In the absence of more detailed information, P-values were assigned to two-digit industries on this basis; these P-values were used to choose the appropriate deviations of actual from optimal wages from Table A-7 and are listed in column 1 of Table A-8. Since we have more detailed information on personnel costs for the Postal Service, the estimate of $2,000 is used to calculate the mean excess wages of 27.4 percent over the years 1958-1972.

The deviations of optimal from actual wages have been calculated for eighteen industries and the Postal Service in order to provide a basis for judging the reliability of the model. That is, this study's conclusions about the Postal Service can be compared with results using the same model for other industries, and further compared with conclusions about the Postal Service garnered from other sources using

Table A-7

MEAN PERCENT DEVIATIONS OF OPTIMAL FROM ACTUAL WAGES, 1958-1972

Industry	Estimated Personnel Costs in 1972					
	$500	$1000	$1500	$2000	$2500	$3000
Postal Service	41.08	34.61	30.49	27.42	24.94	22.86
Machinery, except electrical	18.87	13.60	10.35	7.98	6.09	4.52
Transportation equipment	46.91	39.26	34.29	30.51	27.44	24.82
Apparel & other textile products	32.09	22.13	15.65	10.71	6.69	3.27
Ordnance & accessories	9.33	7.24	6.00	5.10	4.40	3.83
Lumber & wood products	39.39	28.96	22.05	16.74	12.38	8.64
Fabricated metal products	20.02	13.85	10.03	7.21	4.96	3.09
Paper and paper products	19.59	13.54	9.79	7.03	4.83	3.00
Rubber & plastics	12.75	7.56	4.38	2.06	.22	—1.31
Furniture & fixtures	7.13	2.18	—.83	—3.03	—4.77	—6.21
Stone, clay, & glass products	6.23	4.13	2.88	1.98	1.28	.71
Primary metal products	10.11	6.80	4.81	3.37	2.24	1.31
Electrical machinery	5.02	2.02	.22	—1.08	—2.09	—2.93
Instruments & related products	3.47	1.12	—.28	—1.29	—2.08	—2.73
Miscellaneous manufacturing industries	—5.94	—11.25	—14.49	—16.84	—18.69	—20.23
Tobacco & tobacco products	—8.32	—12.59	—15.16	—17.02	—18.49	—19.69
Textile mill products	1.53	—3.78	—7.02	—9.38	—8.91	—12.79
Chemicals & allied products	11.57	7.81	5.53	3.88	2.58	1.51
Leather & leather products	7.05	.61	—3.37	—6.28	—8.60	—10.53

Source: Calculated from Table A-6.

different models. If the results for other industries using the specific human capital model are consistent with results obtained for those industries with other models, then the findings of this study about the Postal Service will be more credible. It is in this spirit, then, that the results for some other industries are examined.

Since 1972 is the most recent year used in this study, a comparison of the results for different industries in this year is particularly useful. The percent deviations of actual from optimal wages for 1972 are listed in Table A-9 for all nineteen industries and for six estimates for personnel costs. The procedure used to assign P-values to two-digit industries for 1972 is the same as that used to assign P-values for

Table A-8

PERCENT DEVIATIONS OF OPTIMAL FROM ACTUAL WAGES

Industry	Mean 1958-1972 (1)	1972 (2)	1958 (3)
Postal Service	27.42	32.55	32.79
Machinery, except electrical	6.09	6.98	8.30
Transportation equipment	24.82	26.34	28.19
Apparel & other textile products	32.09	15.02	35.08
Ordnance & accessories	3.83	0.96	7.18
Lumber & wood products	28.96	30.86	34.26
Fabricated metal products	4.96	7.10	11.58
Paper and paper products	7.03	9.35	10.50
Rubber & plastics	2.06	2.02	7.1
Furniture & fixtures	2.18	1.20	8.2
Stone, clay, & glass products	1.98	6.68	1.16
Primary metal products	1.31	4.13	4.27
Electrical machinery	−1.08	.59	−.35
Instruments & related products	−1.29	−1.47	−.51
Miscellaneous manufacturing industries	−11.25	−10.35	−8.15
Tobacco & tobacco products	−12.59	−.99	−16.60
Textile mill products	1.53	3.6	1.7
Chemicals & allied products	2.58	4.86	2.6
Leather & leather products	7.05	7.59	9.1

Source: Tables A-6 and A-7.

the whole 1958-1972 period. The percent deviations of actual from optimal wages for 1972 calculated on this basis are listed in column 2 of Table A-8. For a value of specific human capital per employee of $2,000, Table A-8 indicates that in 1972 the workers in the Postal Service were "overpaid" by 32.6 percent, more than for any other two-digit industry considered. The next highest value was for workers in the Lumber and wood products industry who were overpaid by 30.86 percent. A negative deviation of actual from optimal wages implies that the workers of the industry were "underpaid." The Miscellaneous manufacturing industries were underpaid the most—10.4 percent.

It is interesting to speculate about the reasons for some industries being "overpaid" and others "underpaid." The estimates of excessive wages in the Lumber and wood products industry might seem rather large in light of the fact that its workers are weakly organized. In this

Table A-9

PERCENT DEVIATION OF OPTIMAL FROM ACTUAL WAGES FOR 1972

Industry	Estimated Personnel Costs					
	$500	$1000	$1500	$2000	$2500	$3000
Postal Service	45.25	39.23	35.41	32.55	30.25	28.31
Machinery, except electrical	19.64	14.42	11.20	8.85	6.98	5.43
Transportation equipment	47.99	40.49	35.62	31.92	28.90	26.34
Apparel & other textile products	31.59	21.56	15.02	10.05	6.00	2.56
Ordnance & accessories	6.07	3.89	2.61	1.68	0.96	0.36
Lumber & wood products	41.01	30.86	24.14	18.97	14.72	11.09
Fabricated metal products	19.92	13.75	9.92	7.09	4.85	2.97
Paper and paper products	21.59	15.69	12.04	9.35	7.20	5.41
Rubber & plastics	10.59	5.27	2.02	−0.36	−2.25	−3.82
Furniture & fixtures	6.19	1.19	−1.85	−4.07	−5.82	−7.28
Stone, clay, & glass products	10.72	8.72	7.53	6.67	6.01	5.46
Primary metal products	12.68	9.47	7.54	6.14	5.04	4.13
Electrical machinery	5.37	2.38	0.59	−0.70	−1.72	−2.55
Instruments & related products	3.31	0.95	−0.46	−1.46	−2.25	−2.91
Miscellaneous manu-facturing industries	−5.08	−10.35	−13.56	−15.89	−17.73	−19.26
Tobacco & tobacco products	6.86	3.19	0.98	−0.61	−1.87	−2.91
Textile mill products	3.59	−1.60	−4.77	−7.08	−8.91	−10.42
Chemicals & allied products	13.64	9.96	7.74	6.13	4.86	3.81
Leather & leather products	7.59	1.19	−2.76	−5.66	−7.96	−9.88

industry voluntary quits are not influenced much by the nonpecuniary aspects of employment as indicated by a relatively low value of $\bar{a}$ in Table A-2. Neither are workers in this industry very sensitive to wage differentials in their decision to quit, as indicated by a relatively low absolute value for $\bar{c}$ in Table A-2. These two considerations together with the assignment of a $1,000 P-value leads to the 30.86 percent estimate of excessive wages in 1972 despite the fact that the quit rate is high. However, if recruitment and training costs in this industry increase disproportionately with high quits, the estimate for the P-value may be too low. If personnel costs were $3,000 per new recruit for the industry, the wages paid in 1972 would be excessive by only 11.09 percent. A more detailed examination of the industry would be required before one could be more specific.

The Transportation and the Primary metals industries are both organized by similar unions and have wage levels that are not dissimilar; yet the model in this study suggests that workers in the Transportation equipment industry are overpaid on average by 25 percent while workers in the Primary metal industry are hardly overpaid at all. Can these results be accounted for? Nonunion barriers to entry may provide the conditions for excessive wages. The degree of government regulation, especially in connection with the Davis-Bacon Act or similar provisions for government contracts, might also be important in explaining excessive wages in the Transportation equipment industry. From Table A-2 the estimate of parameter $\bar{a}$ for workers in Primary metals is 20.5 while for Transportation equipment it is only 0.70. This indicates that workers in the Primary metal products industry have a higher propensity to quit for nonpecuniary reasons and so need to be paid more. On the other hand, the estimate of the parameter $\bar{c}$ for Primary metal products, -18.2, is much larger in absolute magnitude than the estimate for Transportation equipment, -4.15, indicating that workers in the Primary metal products industry are much more sensitive to wage differentials in their decisions to quit. For these reasons, in order to minimize labor costs it might be necessary for employers to pay workers in the Primary metal products industry substantially higher wages than in the Transportation equipment industry; in fact their wage levels are comparable. It follows that employees in the Transportation equipment industry are receiving excessive wages while those in the Primary metals industry are not.

This crude application of the model to highly aggregated two-digit industries does not, of course, *prove* that any of these industries overpay their workers by a *specific percentage*. Perhaps true personnel costs for a particular industry are higher or lower than the estimates used. Perhaps there has been substantial technological progress over the time period examined that has drastically changed the productivity of workers in an industry, their earning power, and consequently personnel costs per new recruit. Perhaps the use of two-digit industries camouflages too much of the detail of individual companies to yield useful results. But even at this crude level of analysis, the model is useful because it separates out some of the important parameters that are helpful in judging wages, suggests the tendency to pay excessive wages in some industries, and provides a basis for assessing some of the wages paid in the economy on the basis of labor response criteria. Most of these qualifications about the use of the model for two-digit industries either do not apply or apply in much reduced force to the Postal Service. I, at least, am persuaded by the evidence produced in

Table A-10

ESTIMATES OF THE EFFECT OF UNIONISM ON
RELATIVE WAGES

Industry	Estimate Date	Percent Deviation of Actual Wages from Optimal Wage Due to Unionism
Contract construction	1939	18
Bituminous coal mining	1956-57	42
Men's clothing manufacturing	1956-57	0
Local transit	1958	12
Hotels	1948	8
Paints and varnishes, footwear, cotton textiles and auto parts manufacturing	1950	0
Wooden furniture, hosiery, and women's dresses manufacturing	1950	7
Barbers	1954	17
Commercial air transportation	1956	24
Seamen	1950s	18
Rubber tire manufacturing	1936-38	13

Source: H. Gregg Lewis, *Unionism and Relative Wages in the United States* (Chicago: University of Chicago Press, 1963), p. 280.

this study and by others that postal workers are overpaid by about *one-third*.

H. Gregg Lewis's study of the effect of unionism on relative wages in the 1950s found that unions raised the relative wages of their members between 10 and 15 percent; and that the average wage of union workers relative to the overall work force was about 7 to 11 percent higher than it would have been in the absence of unionism. It would be interesting to compare these with the average of the mean percentage deviations of optimal from actual wages over the nineteen industries for 1972. From column 2 of Table A-8, I have calculated a weighted average of the means, weighting them by the number of production workers employed in each of the industries.[9] The weighted average, that is, the average deviation of optimal from actual wages over two-digit industries and the Postal Service, is 9.95 percent. Despite the fact that Lewis is measuring slightly different data from a slightly different period, the results are obviously not incompatible.

[9] Employment of production workers for two-digit industries as of May 1972 was taken from *Employment and Earnings*, vol. 19, no. 12 (June 1973), pp. 54-56.

Lewis's estimates of the effect of unionism on wages for certain occupations and groups of industries are listed in Table A-10. Table A-10 shows that the range of the percentage deviations in wages due to union is from 0 for Cotton textiles and Other industries to 42 percent for the Bituminous coal industry, with a mean of 14.45 percent. Unionism was responsible for raising wages 24 percent in the Commercial air transportation industry. Unlike this study, Lewis's study focused primarily on the effects of unionism on wages and neglected other influences. These differing emphases could account not only for the modest difference in findings but also for the possibility that both sets of figures are substantially accurate. Both studies indicate much the same degree of wage excess at the upper end of the scale. The Postal Service in paying about 30 percent more than efficiency criteria would require is at the upper end of the scale according to both Lewis's results and the results of this study.

APPENDIX B

A Review of the Literature on Personnel Costs

Personnel costs are an important variable in the model used in this study for calculating optimal wage levels. The purpose of this appendix is to examine the available accounting estimates of personnel costs in industry in order to judge our estimates for the Postal Service.

Walter Oi developed a study based on a 1951 survey conducted by the International Harvester Company that itemized its estimated personnel costs per new employee, including both hiring and training. The figures generated in his study are listed in Table B-1. The study reestimated fixed employment costs or personnel costs for three job categories: common labor, two-year students, and four-year apprentices. The average total fixed employment cost per new employee estimated by International Harvester was $556.92 in 1951 dollars. Walter Oi revised the training costs downward from $238.40 to $151.36 and lowered International Harvester's estimate of overall personnel costs per new employee to $381.73.

There is an important aspect of personnel costs left out of both International Harvester's and Walter Oi's estimates that tends to make both the estimates low—namely, the loss of productivity from having the inexperienced worker. Neither is there any recognition that a company can choose to some degree between training costs and productivity losses due to employee inexperience. However, higher training costs only tend to mitigate the costs associated with such loss in productivity. Even an expensive training program will not produce fully productive workers overnight. New employees are simply less efficient. For this reason both International Harvester's and Oi's estimates understate the loss in specific human capital when an employee quits. Despite this understatement, the International Harvester estimate is substantial—$556 in 1951 would be the equivalent of

Table B-1

AMOUNT OF MONEY INVESTED PER NEW EMPLOYEE, INTERNATIONAL HARVESTER COMPANY, 1951

Costs	Common Labor	Two-Year Pro-gressive Student	Four-Year Apprentice	IH Average	Revised IH Average
Hiring costs					
Recruiting	$ 4.33	$ 86.38		$ 5.48	$ 5.48
Hiring	13.23	29.08	$ 28.89	13.23	13.91
Orientation	1.56	1.56	1.56	1.56	1.56
Terminating	3.77	3.77	3.77	3.71	3.77
Laying off	1.21	1.21	1.21	1.21	1.21
Recalling	1.30	1.30	1.30	1.30	1.30
Total	25.40	123.30	36.73	26.55	26.51
Training costs					
Training	9.08	11,850.00	18,503.00	238.40	151.36
Tools and materials			164.76	41.19	41.19
Unfilled requisitions	14.92			83.12	24.66
Intrawork transfers	3.50			94.14	64.49
Total	27.50	11,850.00	18,667.76	456.85	281.70
Unemployment compensation	73.52	73.52	73.52	73.52	73.52
Total fixed employment cost	126.42	12,046.82	18,778.01	556.92	381.73

Source: International Harvester Company, "The Cost of Labor Turnover," taken from Walter Y. Oi's "Labor As a Quasi-fixed Factor," *Journal of Political Economy*, December 1962, pp. 538-55.

$1,518 in 1973, adjusted according to the index of average hourly earnings for total private manufacturing.

A 1960 American Management Association research study, *Labor Turnover: Calculation and Costs* by Frederick J. Gaudet, surveys much of the literature investigating personnel costs at the company level. The study reports that in 1958 controllers of eighty companies were asked to estimate the costs of replacing good workers. The nine who replied said that to fill the simplest clerical job, costs would range from $50 to $2,000. In clerical jobs requiring higher skills the estimates ranged from $250 to $7,000.[1] The costs of replacing maintenance workers, high-skill toolmakers, designers, and power plant engineers ranged from $400 to $10,000, with a mean of $1,500. For high-skill maintenance workers like mechanics or stationary engineers, the range was $125 to $6,000, with a mean of $600; for employees in sales and services with technical specialization, $500 to $5,000, with a mean of $1,500; for high-skill employees who required judgment and self-direction, $300 to $2,600, with a mean of $800.[2]

The highest personnel costs are incurred when hiring technical, professional, and managerial employees. William R. Delamater has stated that, conservatively, it would cost $2,000 (in 1972 dollars) to fill lower-level management positions, and $5,000 to $10,000 for technical, sales, and top professionals. He estimated personnel costs for skilled workers at $800 to $1,500; for clerical employees, $300 to $500; and for semiskilled and unskilled workers, under $150.[3] Based on companies of various sizes and types, G. W. Canfield estimated average personnel costs to be slightly under $500 in 1958.

To determine the personnel costs per hire one may look at three general cost categories: recruitment, selection, and placement costs; on-the-job costs; and separation costs. In Table B-2, I have tabulated estimates taken from Gaudet's work for these categories. Recruitment costs shown in section 1 of Table B-2, all calculated per employee hired, include advertising, college recruiting, employment agencies, brochures, booklets, exhibits, prizes and awards to employees, public relations activities, memberships in organizations that aid recruiting, and hotel entertainment. An itemization of these costs in considerable detail, may be found in the original study (see footnote 1 for reference).

---

[1] Frederick J. Gaudet, *Labor Turnover: Calculation and Cost*, AMA Research Study 39 (New York: American Management Association, 1960).

[2] Gaudet, *Labor Turnover*, p. 60. (The figures were generated from a report printed in *Supervisory Management Newsletter*, no. 63 (New York: American Management Association, 1958).

[3] William R. Delamater, *Costs Per Hire* (New York: American Management Association, June 1970).

Table B-2

PERSONNEL COSTS PER EMPLOYEE

(1960 dollars)

	Unskilled		Skilled	Profes-sional
	Laborer	Packer	Technical salesman	Engineer
I. Recruitment costs				
1. Advertising	12	12	375	1650
2. Campus recruiting				1500
3. Employment agency or management search fee				130
4. Brochures, booklets, & exhibits				90
5. Inducements to employees to recruit				65
6. Public relations				5
7. Hotel entertainment				65
8. Public relations literature				80
II. Selection and Placement				
9. Letters of application	4	4	60	50
10. Personnel interviewing	12.50	45	50	67.38
11. Line interviewing	1.00	15	8	25
12. Medical examination	7.08	8	10	10
13. Reference checks	10	15	35	35
14. Security and credit investigation			50	
15. Psychological testing	2	3	240	
16. Travel				65
17. Personnel department overhead	25	25	25	
III. On-the-job costs				
18. Bookkeeping operations	3	3	10	20
19. Paraphernalia	15	15	20	35
20. Orientation program	18	18	45	450
21. Indoctrination	5	5	25	25
22. Training programs				
23. Break-in costs	100	100	200	200
24. Overtime costs				

	Unskilled		Skilled	Profes- sional
	Laborer	Packer	Technical salesman	Engineer
IV. Separation costs				
25. Exit interviews	3	3	10	20
26. Extra social security taxes	10	10	10	15
27. Extra unemployment insurance costs	10	10	15	
28. Loss of good will and lowered morale	30	30	50	200
29. TOTAL	267.58	321	1238	4802.38
30. TOTALa (1972 dollars)	$471.00	$565	$2179	$8452

a The index of average hourly earnings for workers in total private manufacturing was used to convert 1960 dollars to 1972 dollars. See *Employment and Earnings*, vol. 20, no. 8 (February 1974), Table C-12. The multiplier is 1.76.

Source: Compiled from estimates in Frederick J. Gaudet, *Labor Turnover: Calculation and Costs*, AMA Research Study 39 (New York: American Management Association, Inc., 1960).

In line 29 of Table B-2 I have added up all the items contributing to the personnel costs per new hire in 1960 dollars. In line 30 I have used the index of average hourly wages for total private employment to adjust the 1960 dollars to 1972 dollars. Using the figures generated from this table for an unskilled worker, the personnel costs per hire are approximately $518; for a skilled worker, $2,179; for a professional, $8,452. These figures are merely representative, of course. Not all firms have personnel programs in all the areas mentioned and some may have programs in areas not covered here. However, these estimates, especially for unskilled workers ($561) and for skilled workers ($2,315), seem to provide excellent guidelines for evaluating personnel costs in the Postal Service and in other industries.

BIBLIOGRAPHY

Allan, Keven, and Reed, Graham L. (eds.). *Nationalized Industries.* Baltimore: Penguin Books, 1970.

Allen, Frederick. "The Post Office Has Problems." *The Atlanta Constitution,* October 24, 1973.

American Enterprise Institute for Public Policy Research. *Postal Reforms Proposals,* June 8, 1970.

Armknect, Paul A., and Early, John F. "Quits in Manufacturing—A Study of Their Causes." *Monthly Labor Review,* November 1972, pp. 31-36.

"As Economy Surges Acute Labor Shortage Plagues Many Areas." *Wall Street Journal,* June 21, 1973.

Ashenfelter, Orley. "The Effect of Unionization on Wages in the Public Sector: The Case of Firefighters." *Industrial and Labor Relations Review,* vol. 24, no. 2, January 1971, pp. 191-202.

Baratz, Morton S. *The Economics of the Postal Service.* Washington, D.C.: Public Affairs Press, 1962.

Becker, G. S. *Human Capital.* New York: National Bureau of Economic Research, 1966.

Behman, Sarah. "Labor Mobility—Increasing Labor Demand and Money Wage Rate Increases in U.S. Manufacturing." *Review of Economic Studies,* vol. 31, October 1964, pp. 253-66.

Brownlee, K. A. *Statistical Theory and Methodology in Science and Engineering.* New York: John Wiley and Sons, 1965.

Brozen, Yale. "Wage Rates, Minimum Wage Laws, and Unemployment." *New Individualist Review,* vol. 4, no. 3, Spring 1966, pp. 24-33.

————. "The New Competition—International Markets: How Should We Adapt?" *Journal of Business of the University of Chicago,* vol. 33, no. 4, October 1960, pp. 322-26.

Burton, John R., Jr. "Reply." *Industrial and Labor Relations Review,* vol. 23, no. 1, 1969, pp. 84-88.

———— and Parker, John E. "Interindustry Variations in Voluntary Labor Mobility." *Industrial and Labor Relations Review,* vol. 22, no. 2, January 1969, pp. 199-216.

————. "There Is a New Industrial Feudalism." Unpublished manuscript, Chicago, n.d.

————. "Voluntary Labor Mobility in the U.S. Manufacturing Sector." *Proceedings of the Industrial Relations Research Association,* Winter 1967, pp. 61-70.

Carlson, Robert J., and Robinson, James W. "Toward a Public Employment Wage Theory." *Industrial and Labor Relations Review,* vol. 22, January 1969, pp. 243-48.

Chamberlain, Neil W. *The Labor Sector.* New York: McGraw-Hill, 1965.

Chambers, Jay. "A Theoretical Model of Resource Allocation by the Public School District: A Formal Representation." Unpublished manuscript, Berkeley, 1972.

————. "Teachers' Unions, Collective Negotiations, and Resource Allocation in Public School Districts." Unpublished manuscript, Berkeley, 1972.

————. "The Impact of Teachers' Negotiations: The Empirical Results." Unpublished manuscript, Berkeley, 1972.

Cohen, R., and McBride, C. "Sorting Mechanization Requirements for Large, Medium and Small Post Offices." Paper presented at the 44th National Meeting of the Operations Research Society of America, November 14, 1973.

Ehrenberg, R. G. "Municipal Government Structure, Unionization, and the Wages of Firefighters." *Industrial Labor Relations Review,* vol. 27, no. 1, October 1973, pp. 36-48.

Ewing, Donald R., and Salaman, Roger K. *The Postal Crisis: The Postal Function As a Communications Service.* Washington, D.C.: U.S. Department of Commerce/Office of Telecommunications, January 1977.

Fogle, Walter, and Lewin, David. "Public Sector Wage Determination." Research Paper No. 30, Graduate School of Business, Columbia University, New York, 1974.

Gallaway, Lowell E. "Inter-Industry Labor Mobility among Men, 1957-1960." *Social Security Bulletin,* vol. 29, no. 9, September 1966.

Gaudet, Frederick. *Labor Turnover: Calculation and Costs.* New York: American Management Association, 1960.

Gentry, Margaret. "Rise Allowed in Mail Rates." *Washington Post,* September 1, 1973.

Haldi, John, with Johnston, Joseph F., Jr. *Postal Monopoly: An Assessment of the Private Express Statutes.* Washington, D.C.: American Enterprise Institute for Public Policy Research, 1974.

Horsefield, J. K. "Some Notes on Postal Finance." *Bulletin of the Oxford Institute of Economics and Statistics,* vol. 26, 1964, pp. 39-58. Reprinted in *Public Enterprise,* ed. R. Turvey. Baltimore: Penguin Books, 1968.

Joseph, Frank. "Postal Report: Administration Victorious in Long Fight for Basic Reform of Postal System." *CPR National Journal,* July 4, 1970, pp. 1434-36.

Kappel Commission. *Towards Postal Excellence.* Report of the President's Commission on Postal Organization, vols. 1-5. Washington, D.C., 1968.

Kennedy, Jane. "Structure and Policy in Postal Rates." *Journal of Political Economy,* vol. 45, no. 3, June 1957, pp. 185-208.

Kerr, Willard, and Smith, Frank J. "The Exit Interview." *Journal of Applied Psychology,* vol. 37, no. 5, October 1953, pp. 352-55.

"Labor—The Quiet Front," *Newsweek,* July 30, 1973, p. 57.

Lester, Richard A. *Economics of Labor.* New York: Macmillan Co., 1964.

Lewis, H. Gregg. *Unionism and Relative Wages in the United States.* Chicago: University of Chicago Press, 1963.

Lurie, Melvin, "Government Regulation and Union Power: A Case Study of the Boston Transit Industry." *Journal of Law and Economics,* vol. 3, October 1960, pp. 122-35.

Mantell, Edmund H. "Factors Affecting Labor Productivity in Post Offices." *Journal of the American Statistical Association,* vol. 69, no. 346, June 1974, Applications Section, pp. 303-9.

Merewitz, L. "Costs and Returns to Scale in U.S. Post Offices." *Journal of the American Statistical Association,* vol. 66, no. 335, September 1971, pp. 504-9.

Meyer, Charles A. "Patterns of Labor Mobility." *Manpower in the U.S.: Problems and Policies.* New York: Harper and Brothers, 1954.

Mincer, Jacob. *Schooling, Experience and Earnings.* New York: National Bureau of Economic Research, 1974.

Mossberg, Walter. "Postal Service Is Told to Cut Rates on First-Class Mail, Boost Others." *Wall Street Journal,* May 29, 1975.

———. "Study Backs Closing 57% of Post Offices, But No Immediate Plans Made to Do So." *Wall Street Journal,* May 9, 1977.

————. "Postal Service Is Losing Out on R & D." *Wall Street Journal*, May 10, 1977.

Myers, Robert J. *The Coming Collapse of the Post Office.* Englewood Cliffs, N.J.: Prentice-Hall, 1975.

Niskanen, William A., Jr. *Bureaucracy and Representative Government.* Chicago and New York: Aldine-Atherton, 1971.

Oi, Walter Y. "Labor As a Quasi-Fixed Factor." *Journal of Political Economy*, vol. 70, December 1962, pp. 538-55.

The Organization for Economic Cooperation and Development. *Wages and Labor Mobility.* Paris: OECD, 1965.

Parnes, Herbert S. "The Labor Force and Labor Markets." In Herbert G. Heneman, Jr. et al., eds., *Employment Relations Research.* New York: Harper and Brothers, 1960, pp. 16-33.

Perloff, Steven H. "Comparing Municipal Salaries with Industry and Federal Pay." *Monthly Labor Review*, vol. 94, October 1971, pp. 46-50.

Postmaster General. *Annual Report of the Postmaster General, 1972-1973.* Washington, D.C., 1973.

————. *Annual Report of the Postmaster General, 1973-1974.* Washington, D.C., 1974.

————. *Annual Report of the Postmaster General, 1974-1975.* Washington, D.C., 1975.

————. *Annual Report of the Postmaster General, Fiscal 1976 and Transition Quarter.* Washington, D.C., 1976.

"Postal Reorganization Act." *Legislative History*, pp. 3649-70.

"Postal Service at One Year, Still a Long Way to Go." *National Report.* Washington, D.C.: Congressional Quarterly, Inc., 1972.

"Postal Unions Worry about Big City Revolt in This Week's Contract Vote." *Wall Street Journal*, July 17, 1973, p. 1.

Rees, Albert. "Information Networks in Labor Markets." *American Economic Review*, vol. 56, May 1966, pp. 559-66.

Reynolds, Alan. "A Kind Word for 'Cream Skimming.'" *Harvard Business Review*, vol. 52, November-December 1974.

Rich, Wesley Everett. *The History of the United States Post Office to the Year 1829.* Cambridge: Harvard University Press, 1924.

Rottenberg, Simon. "On Choice in Labor Markets." *Industrial and Labor Relations Review*, vol. 9, no. 2, January 1956, pp. 183-214.

"Senate Votes to Create Independent Postal Service." *National Report.* Washington, D.C.: Congressional Quarterly, Inc., 1970.

Simons, H. C. "Some Reflections on Syndicalism." *Economic Policy for a Free Society.* Chicago: University of Chicago Press, 1948.

Smith, Adam. *The Wealth of Nations*, ed. E. Cannon. New York: Random House, 1937.

Smith, Sharon P. "Wages in the Postal Service." Working Paper No. 68, Industrial Relations Section, Princeton University, April 1975.

Stans, Maurice H. "Financial Reorganization in the U.S. Post Office." *Journal of Accountancy*, June 1957, pp. 53-59.

———. "Financial Reorganization in the U.S. Post Office, Part II." *Journal of Accountancy*, July 1957, pp. 33-44.

Stigler, George J. "Information in the Labor Market." *Journal of Political Economy*, vol. 70, no. 5, part 2, Supplement, October 1962, pp. 94-105.

Telser, Lester G. *Competition, Collusion and Game Theory*. Chicago and New York: Aldine-Atherton, 1972.

———. "Concentration Ratios—What Do They Signify." Unpublished manuscript, November 1971.

Thorpe, Ruth E. "Postal Report, Mail Unions and Government Enter Era of Collective Bargaining." *CPR National Journal*, December 5, 1970, pp. 2655-60.

Tiedemann, J. G. "Study Analyzing Four City Post Offices, Particularly Their Resignation Rates." (Privately circulated), 1969.

———. "Average Personnel Costs for Recruiting Testing, Hiring, Training." (Privately circulated), 1967.

Ullman, L. "Labor Mobility and the Industrial Wage Structure in the Post-War United States." *Quarterly Journal of Economics*, vol. 79, no. 1, February 1965, pp. 73-97.

U.S. Department of Justice. *Changing the Private Express Laws, Competitive Alternatives and the U.S. Postal Service*. Washington, D.C., January 1977.

U.S. Post Office Department, Office of the General Counsel. *Restriction on Transportation of Letters—The Private Express Statutes and Interpretations*, 5th ed., May 1972.

U.S. Post Office Department. *Internal Audit Report*, Review of Employees' Separations and Turnover, Phase II, January 1966 to May 1967. Internal Audit Division, Bureau of the Chief Postal Inspector.

U.S. Postal Service. Agreement between the U.S. Postal Service and American Postal Workers Union, AFL-CIO, National Association of Letter Carriers, AFL-CIO, National Post Office Mail Handlers, Watchmen, Messengers and Group Leaders, Division of Labor International Union of North America, AFL-CIO, National Rural Letter Carriers Association, July 21, 1973, to July 30, 1975.

———. *Budget of the United States Postal Service FY 1978*. As submitted to the Office of Management and Budget pursuant to 39 U.S.C. 2009. December 14, 1976.

————. *Comprehensive Statement of Postal Operations.* Presented to the Committees on Post Office and Civil Service and the Committees on Appropriations of the Senate and the House of Representatives pursuant to 39 U.S.C. 2401(g), as added by P.L. No. 94-421. 1977.

————. *National Payroll Hour Summary Report.* Fiscal year, June 26, 1971, to June 23, 1972.

————. "Pay Scales in the Postal Service," April 1973.

————. *The Postal Service Manual.*

U.S. Postal Service Board of Governors. *The Private Express Statutes and Their Administration.* Washington, D.C., 1973.

U.S., Congress, House of Representatives, Committee on the Post Office and Civil Service, Subcommittee on Postal Operations and Service. *Proceedings, Hearing on Oversight of the United States Postal Service.* 95th Congress, 1st session, March 15, 1977.

U.S., Senate, Committee on Post Office and Civil Service. *Explanation of the Postal Reorganization Act and Selected Background Material.* July 1973, pp. 1-3, 14, 15, 21, 156-58, 169, 241, 248.

Wattles, George M. "Rates and Costs of the United States Postal Service," *Journal of Law and Economics,* vol. 16, no. 7, April 1973, pp. 89-117.